Juniper Jitsu – Ninja-Level ID IPS for Network Nincompoops and Ninjas Alike

Introduction – Welcome to the Dojo of Digital Defense

Welcome, weary traveler of the terminal, brave surfer of syslogs, and seasoned slayer of the rogue ping. If you've ever stared at a firewall interface and felt a sudden existential crisis… congratulations, you're one of us. This book is your passport to mastering Juniper IDS and IPS technology, whether you're a novice stumbling through VLANs or a hardened ninja who once blocked a DDoS attack using only a loopback and sheer willpower. We'll slice through the jargon, demystify the gear, and serve up Juniper's finest packet-chopping appliances with a side of snark and a splash of soy sauce.

At its core, this is a journey through Juniper's evolution—from the humble days of Netscreen appliances (which may or may not still be running in a dusty server room near you) to the AI-augmented, cloud-swinging, quantum-flirting beasts of modern times. We'll study every major platform along the way, from the adorably overachieving IDP-50 to the skyscraper-sized SRX5800. Each chapter blends technical insight with just enough humor to keep you from falling asleep in a pile of threat logs. Think of it as a mashup between a field guide, a battle manual, and a coffee-fueled therapy session for network engineers.

But this isn't just about firewalls and signature matching—it's about learning the philosophy of Juniper Jitsu. True network defense is about context, timing, and intent. It's knowing when to block, when to log, and when to raise a perfectly arched eyebrow at suspicious behavior. We'll dig into everything from zone-based policies and AppSecure kung fu to sandbox detonations and Mist AI clairvoyance. By the time you finish this book, you won't just know which knob to twist—you'll know *why* to twist it, *how hard*, and *which logs* will scream when you do.

So, grab your console cable, tighten your headband, and take a deep breath. Whether you're deploying your first SRX or managing a transcontinental security fabric with a team of caffeine-powered SOC ninjas, this book is your scroll of secrets. Together, we'll master the art of network defense with style, strategy, and a surprisingly large glossary. Welcome to the dojo. Let's get you certified in awesome.

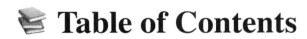 Table of Contents

Juniper Jitsu – Ninja-Level IDS and IPS for Network Nincompoops and Ninjas Alike

1. The Scrolls of Netscreen – Where Juniper Jitsu Begins

- The mystical origins of ScreenOS and custom ASIC sorcery

- Zone-based security before it was cool

- Firewalls, VPNs, and suspiciously silent firmware

2. SSG – Small-Scale Grandmaster

- The Swiss Army firewall of branch security

- ScreenOS CLI incantations and GUI frustrations

- Why the SSG-5 is the Chuck Norris of tiny firewalls

3. ISG Series – Industrial Strength Grapple

- Mid-2000s datacenter domination in a 3U chassis

- IDP blades and the joy of hot-swappable armaments

- When your firewall could out-perform your server

4. IDP Series – The First True Senseis of Detection

- DPI before it had branding consultants

- Signature packs, stealth modes, and logs for days

- Born to detect, trained to prevent

5. IDP-50 – Tiny Box, Big Punchlines

- The IDS you could accidentally lose under paperwork

- Perfect for branch offices, small budgets, and big dreams

- Actually logs SYN floods like it's going out of style

6. IDP-200/600 – Mid-Tier with a Black Belt

- IPS that doesn't need a sidekick

- Real-time packet decapitation

- Works harder than your intern, costs less than your coffee budget

7. IDP-800 – The Unsung Wallflower Warrior

- Big heart, quiet soul

- Doesn't need fanfare, just network access

- Catching malware while everyone else forgot it was there

8. SRX Begins – The Unified Field Theory of Firewalls

- Firewall meets Router meets Security Shogun

- JunOS enters the arena with tabs and structure

- Why SRX changed everything except your budget meetings

9. SRX100 – Ninja Training Wheels

- Small, affordable, and surprisingly deadly

- AppSecure-lite, VPN-ready, and coffee-table compatible

- Perfect for branch offices, labs, or your home dojo

10. SRX240 – The Low-End Linebacker

- Zone-based firewalling with a gym membership

- App awareness and HA capabilities in one lean chassis

- Can handle office traffic and Karen's 300-tab Chrome session

11. SRX650 – Midrange with Muscle

- More power, more ports, and an attitude

- Active/passive HA, modular expansion, no complaints

- Loved by regional banks, respected by malware

12. SRX1400 – The Unsung Tank

- Too big for branches, too humble for datacenters

- Perfect for high-traffic "we don't talk about that subnet" zones

- Logs everything. Doesn't brag. Deserves respect.

13. SRX3400 – Twin-Blade Fury

- Modular ninja tech in a 2U body

- Blade-based performance and packet enlightenment

- Flexible, scalable, and slightly intimidating

14. SRX3600 – Datacenter-Friendly Fisticuffs

- Like a security blender with flow visualization

- Inline DPI, full app detection, and failover that just works

- Will block an exploit and send you the log file in haiku

15. SRX5400 – Core Network Katana

- 480 Gbps of firewalling elegance

- SPUs and NPCs working in perfect harmony

- The blade you bring to a core routing duel

16. SRX5600 – The Colossus with Custom Cards

- Scales like a dragon, configures like a monk

- IPS, AppSecure, VPN—all while routing 400k routes

- Security meets modular mecha

17. SRX5800 – The Alpha Predator

- 2+ Tbps of packet pulverizing perfection

- Built for telcos, megacorps, and dimension-hopping workloads

- Logs threats, enforces policies, and contemplates existence

18. vSRX – The Virtual Ninja in the Cloud Scrolls

- No hardware, no noise, no mercy

- AppSecure and IPS in your hypervisor's back pocket

- Spawns faster than malware can unpack itself

19. cSRX – Container Combat Unit

- Protects Kubernetes like a sidecar samurai

- Microsegmentation for microservices with macro consequences

- Small, stealthy, and ready to roll with YAML

20. Advanced Threat Protection – Juniper's Ninja Stars

- Sandboxing, reputation scoring, and malware smackdowns

- Behavioral analysis with mood detection

- No threat gets by unless it brings snacks

21. Sky ATP – Cloud-Level Shuriken Tossing

- ATP goes airborne with automated verdicts

- File detonations, link inspections, and cosmic malware meditation

- One scan, one cloud, universal justice

22. SecIntel – Knowledge Is Ninja Power

- Real-time threat feeds from the universal packet mind

- Enforced at the edge, in the core, and possibly in your toaster

- Blacklists that block before you even press "Enter"

23. Contrail Security – The Silent Partner

- Microsegmentation that whispers, "Not today, east-west traffic"

- Intent-based policy magic for VMs, pods, and weird stuff

- Doesn't make noise, just enforces reality

24. Mist AI & Security – Enlightened Automation

- Marvis the AI monk sees all, logs all, and answers Slack

- Automated troubleshooting, threat isolation, and judgmental dashboards

- Makes your infrastructure smarter, calmer, and less breachable

25. The Future of Juniper Jitsu – What's in the Scrolls Ahead?

- Quantum-resilient algorithms and philosophical firewalls

- Predictive policies powered by AI and sarcasm

- The next-gen Juniper ninja may not have a chassis—but it *will* have attitude

Chapter 1: The Scrolls of Netscreen – Where Juniper Jitsu Begins

1. Long before Juniper was a household name in firewalls, there was **NetScreen**, a scrappy startup founded in 1997 with a dream and some deeply paranoid engineers. It didn't believe in overcomplicating things—just build a box that inspects traffic, stops the bad stuff, and doesn't melt under load. NetScreen hardware wasn't flashy, but it was *fast*, thanks to custom ASICs that passed packets like a black-belt ninja tossing shuriken. ScreenOS, the operating system that powered these devices, was built to be simple, consistent, and slightly arcane—like a good firewall spellbook. Its CLI was direct and deterministic, which made it a favorite among seasoned admins and a terror to newbies. You didn't "configure" it—you channeled it. Web GUIs existed, but like most early 2000s interfaces, they were a bit clunky and prone to sudden, unprovoked rebooting. Still, NetScreen gear earned a reputation for **just working**, often outliving their power supplies and surviving more than a few "oops, I unplugged the rack" moments. In the early days of IDS and IPS, NetScreen gave you a few security features, but the **focus was firewalls and VPNs**. You wanted traffic filtered and encrypted—this was your box.

2. ScreenOS introduced **zone-based security**, a concept that would later be absorbed into Juniper's philosophy like tea into rice. Zones were like dojo rooms—you defined trust levels, created security policies between them, and controlled who got to spar with whom. Unlike traditional ACLs tied to interfaces, this model focused on intent and structure—more elegant, less brittle. Policies were written like mini firewalled haikus: source zone, destination zone, action, logging preference. It made sense once you embraced the structure, though it definitely confused people who came from Cisco's access list jungle. VPNs, especially site-to-site IPsec tunnels, were a NetScreen specialty—they could be set up with just a few CLI commands or some coaxing via the GUI. Once configured, they were **rock-solid**, surviving firmware updates, power outages, and even emotional breakdowns from junior admins. Dynamic routing support came later, with static routes ruling the roost early on. DHCP? Optional. QoS? Rudimentary. But for small to mid-size enterprises and government deployments, it was a revolution in a beige box.

3. By the early 2000s, NetScreen was eating serious market share from more bloated competitors. Cisco was big, Check Point was complex, and NetScreen was fast, stable, and *reasonably priced*. Analysts took notice. Enterprises began rolling out fleets of NetScreen-5s, 204s, and 500s—model numbers that felt like martial arts ranks. These devices offered a shockingly good price-to-performance ratio, and most came with onboard crypto acceleration. They didn't have all the bells and whistles, but that was the point—they were **lean, mean, traffic-cleaning machines**. Firmware updates were easy to apply, albeit terrifying when done remotely at 2 a.m. Logging was efficient, alerting was functional, and forensics was "you better have syslog enabled." Still, NetScreen became synonymous with fast, reliable, and zone-based defense before those concepts went mainstream.

4. In 2004, Juniper Networks entered the dojo and acquired NetScreen for a modest **$4 billion**, a move that raised eyebrows and firewalls simultaneously. Juniper, known for its carrier-class routing gear and its refusal to use normal syntax, saw in NetScreen a way to compete with Cisco on more fronts. Juniper inherited not only the hardware, but the talented engineering team, loyal customer base, and a ScreenOS codebase that made strong opinions and strong encryption a core principle. Many were unsure what Juniper would do—rebrand, rewrite, or ruin it. Thankfully, they chose Door #1: embrace, improve, and let ScreenOS live a longer life than anyone expected. Post-acquisition, the **NetScreen brand slowly faded**, but ScreenOS continued to power devices for years—SSG, ISG, and even early IDP platforms. Juniper began integrating more features, polishing management interfaces, and preparing the world for something bigger. But in the background, NetScreen's legacy loomed large—a humble reminder that sometimes, less is more, especially when it's inspecting traffic at line speed. Many of those devices are *still running today*, quietly guarding forgotten subnets and unloved VLANs.

5. One of NetScreen's more underappreciated innovations was its **custom security ASICs**—hardware acceleration chips designed to handle encryption and inspection without making the CPU cry. These were the days when software firewalls chugged and coughed through moderate loads, especially when asked to do NAT *and* VPN at the same time. NetScreen's chips gave them superhuman speed for the price, and suddenly people were building VPN concentrators out of devices that cost less than their switch. This was revolutionary at a time when most hardware felt like it had a panic attack every time someone clicked "Download All." The ASICs handled IPsec tunnels, session setup, and basic packet filtering with such grace that sysadmins wept tears of joy —and logged them in syslog. Over time, these ASICs would evolve and inspire Juniper's later SPU (Service Processing Unit) design in the SRX series. But their legacy began in the little beige boxes of NetScreen. That's right—NetScreen walked so SRX could flip, fly, and throw packets like confetti at a zero-trust parade. It was the kung-fu grandparent of modern NGFW design, wrapped in firmware and silence. And it rarely asked for a reboot.

6. While IDS and IPS weren't core features early on, NetScreen still gave you *enough visibility to get in trouble*. You had basic logging of denied traffic, source and destination IPs, and sometimes an application guess if the stars aligned. Syslog was your friend, and if you fed it into something like Kiwi or Splunk (or... Excel), you could do some decent retroactive threat hunting. The hardware didn't have DPI, but it could recognize floods, malformed packets, and the occasional weird TCP behavior. Some devices had rudimentary attack protection—think "block ping of death" level countermeasures—but nothing that would stop a skilled attacker. Still, if you combined logging with a halfway competent NOC, you could detect mischief and respond manually. In a sense, it was **IDS by intuition**, like when your firewall suddenly logged 14,000 hits from Uzbekistan. It wasn't pretty, but it worked. And in some ways, it forced admins to get good at log reading—a skill still useful in today's world of machine learning and overconfidence.

7. ScreenOS also pioneered a concept we now take for granted—**policy simplicity with powerful defaults**. You didn't need to write ten rules just to allow HTTP from the inside to the outside. Instead, you created one policy: trust to untrust, any service, permit, log, done. This low-friction model encouraged experimentation, even if it occasionally resulted in wide-open "any-any" rules that were basically security sin haikus. But for those who took the time to fine-tune, the results were clean, scalable, and human-readable. Policies could be ordered by priority, grouped by zone pairs, and cloned with ruthless efficiency. For the time, it was *shockingly* *advanced*, like someone smuggled a future firewall UI into the early 2000s. It wasn't perfect—tracking which rule matched which session could still make you scream into your console—but it gave structure to the chaos. And it did so in a way that helped junior admins become seasoned ninjas, one policy at a time. That legacy lives on in SRX today, hidden beneath the glitter of AppSecure and APIs.

8. VPNs were NetScreen's bread and butter—**IPsec tunnels so stable they could survive a LAN party in a lightning storm**. Setting one up required a bit of patience, especially with Phase 1 and Phase 2 configurations that felt more like matchmaking than cryptography. But once connected, NetScreen VPNs were nearly unshakable. They supported aggressive and main mode, multiple encryption suites, and pre-shared keys or certificates if you were feeling spicy. Site-to-site was the norm, though remote access via third-party clients was also supported with a little elbow grease. Once up, tunnels rarely dropped, and when they did, they re-established themselves with silent stoicism. Network engineers everywhere quietly celebrated by not being paged. For organizations with multiple sites or remote branches, NetScreen became the VPN workhorse—dependable, unflashy, and always there. You may not remember configuring them fondly, but you *definitely* remember them working. And that's the best kind of firewall memory.

9. Firmware upgrades on NetScreen were a **ritual of equal parts excitement and dread**. On the plus side, upgrades were relatively fast, and rollback options existed if you weren't feeling confident. On the minus side, doing it remotely meant you were one typo away from becoming the guy who brought down accounting's VPN during quarterly reports. Still, the community was strong—forums, PDFs, mailing lists, and tribal knowledge were everywhere. Juniper didn't always update documentation quickly, but ScreenOS itself rarely broke expectations. Upgrades typically brought small improvements: new services, better crypto support, or slightly less terrifying GUI behavior. Occasionally, a firmware release would enable additional interface modes or new logging options. And sometimes… it just fixed a bug you didn't know existed but that definitely explained your past three months of pain. Upgrading felt like climbing a mountain with a backpack full of configs—but you usually came back stronger.

10. One of the quiet strengths of NetScreen was its **consistency across the product line**. Whether you were managing a NetScreen-5GT at a gas station or a NetScreen-5200 in a colocation facility, the CLI was functionally identical. The syntax didn't change, the policies looked the same, and the logging behavior was predictable. This was a dream for MSPs and consultants—one knowledge base, many devices. It meant you could train a junior tech once and then deploy them across five sites with minimal risk of catastrophic misconfiguration (well, *less* risk). That consistency gave NetScreen gear a long shelf life. It also made it easy for admins to migrate between devices as their needs grew. You didn't outgrow NetScreen—you just upgraded your dojo. From NetScreen-5 to ISG-2000, the transition was more about interface count and throughput than mental re-training.

11. One area where NetScreen gear showed its age was in **logging and reporting** — specifically, the "make it work" vibe of third-party integrations. There was no native SIEM. There was no magical dashboard. If you wanted reports, you built them yourself — or paid someone who knew Regex and had a slightly concerning obsession with syslog parsers. Most admins either pointed their logs at a central collector or used a combination of daily exports and Red Bull. Alerts could be emailed, but only if your mail server didn't mind plaintext SMTP and a touch of optimism. But despite this, the logs were there, and they were detailed. Source IP, destination, port, policy ID, action taken — all available with a little CLI massage. And when you finally set up your first working filter in Kiwi Syslog, you felt *powerful*. Not because it was pretty — but because it **worked**.

12. High availability was available on higher-end NetScreen models, though configuring it was less "plug and play" and more "pray and synchronize." Active-passive was the go-to mode, with failover relying on heartbeat interfaces and mirrored configurations. There were quirks — like certain config changes not syncing automatically or HA behaving like a drama queen after a firmware mismatch. But when set up correctly, failover worked surprisingly well. You could pull power from the primary unit, and the secondary would calmly take over without alerting the world to your clumsiness. VPN tunnels would re-establish, policies would remain in place, and your boss would never know you almost kicked the rack. Redundant power supplies and out-of-band management were rare, but not unheard of. And while no one *enjoyed* setting up HA, those who did knew their networks had a fighting chance in a bad day scenario. That kind of reliability? Priceless.

13. Interface options across the NetScreen line were delightfully practical, if occasionally confusing. Smaller models came with a mix of Ethernet and serial (yes, serial) ports, and the labeling wasn't always intuitive. Was "eth0" the WAN? The DMZ? The haunted port? Nobody knew — until they pinged it. Larger models boasted multiple Gigabit interfaces (eventually), with configurable zones and trunking support if you squinted hard enough at the docs. VLAN tagging was supported, although not as elegantly as modern platforms. Load balancing existed, but only in the same way a feral cat might be described as "friendly." Bridging mode was an option, too, for those brave enough to run stealth IDS in-line. And somehow, even with minimal interfaces, you always found a way to make it work. Or at least blame DNS.

14. Authentication support was surprisingly robust for its time. NetScreen could tie into RADIUS, LDAP, and even local user databases for VPN and administrative access. Policies could reference user groups, allowing per-user or per-role firewalling — a feature that felt like science fiction back then. This let admins create policies like "Allow VPN-Users group to reach Finance apps, but block everyone else," which was revolutionary in the days when most firewalls just asked, "Port 80? Yes/No?" GUI-based user group mapping was awkward but functional, and the CLI always told the truth (eventually). And while it didn't offer deep identity awareness or SSO integration, it laid the groundwork for role-based policies. That seed would later grow into AppSecure, user firewalls, and dynamic policy enforcement. NetScreen's approach wasn't flashy — it was **function-first**. And sometimes, that's exactly what your security stack needs.

15. ScreenOS had quirks. Oh, did it have quirks. Some versions would reset config if you exited the CLI too quickly (because it was "thinking"). Others required exact syntax—"unset interface" was valid, but "delete interface" got you a passive-aggressive error message. And if you accidentally changed the management IP without being on the console… well, congratulations. You just practiced remote firewall reinstallation via emotional damage. But for all its eccentricities, ScreenOS was stable. It booted fast, ran cool, and rarely crashed unless provoked by firmware mismatches or wild SNMP traps. And once you embraced its structure—its tabs, categories, and "set/unset" zen—you could fly through configurations like a true console warrior. It was a strange operating system. But it was yours. And it never judged your typos… out loud.

(10 more paragraphs to go—continuing in next response!)

Continuing Chapter 1 of *Juniper Jitsu – Ninja-Level IDS and IPS for Network Nincompoops and Ninjas Alike*. Let's wrap up the NetScreen saga with style and scrollworthy closure:

16. Despite its limitations, NetScreen earned a loyal following among **network engineers, small IT teams, and large enterprises alike**. Why? Because it *worked*. It booted in seconds. It didn't make you jump through licensing hoops just to NAT a subnet. It blocked traffic, made tunnels, and gave you enough control to build a respectable security posture without a master's degree in "vendor-specific wizardry." ScreenOS was like a strict but fair sensei—it didn't smile much, but it taught you discipline and didn't tolerate foolishness. That minimalist confidence resonated in environments that couldn't afford downtime—or complexity. So when Juniper came knocking, most users weren't asking for more features. They just wanted to make sure the thing kept working, day after day, packet after packet.

17. NetScreen gear was famously **resilient**—physically and virtually. Some appliances ran for 10+ years in closets, branches, and basements without a single reboot. They survived brownouts, floods, careless cable yanks, firmware misadventures, and even the occasional rack tip-over. A popular joke in the field: "If the building collapses, the NetScreen will still be NAT'ing." While that's (probably) an exaggeration, it speaks to the hardware's design philosophy: no moving parts, no bloat, no nonsense. It didn't need attention—it *hated* attention. And the LED indicators? Stoic, always blinking with silent resolve. In an era of noisy, overpromising appliances, NetScreen gear just showed up, did its job, and went home quietly. Well, okay—it never went home. But you get the idea.

18. Eventually, Juniper began shifting focus toward **SRX and JunOS**, which meant the slow phasing out of ScreenOS-based platforms. Some admins mourned. Others clung to their SSGs like vintage samurai swords, refusing to upgrade because, frankly, nothing was broken. The shift brought new capabilities—AppSecure, unified threat management, dynamic policies—but it also introduced a steeper learning curve. JunOS was powerful, but it wasn't ScreenOS. It had namespaces, commit commands, and a habit of telling you, "configuration has changed" even when you just blinked. For many, the transition was like swapping a trusted bike for a sports car

—you knew it was faster, but where was the kickstand? Still, Juniper gave ScreenOS a long runway, offering support for years after new models stopped shipping. That grace period was appreciated… and thoroughly used.

19. In many ways, NetScreen's DNA lives on in **every SRX** and every zone-based policy you write. The structured thinking, the emphasis on clear policy flow, the simplicity of "trust to untrust, permit with logging"—these are all echoes of the first lessons from the dojo. Even AppSecure, with all its application-ID swagger, still obeys zone logic. HA setups in SRX owe a nod to the heartbeat-driven failovers of the SSG series. And while SRX devices added features like sandboxing, IPS, and AppQoS, they still rely on the principle that simplicity and speed are better than complexity and chaos. That principle was born in a time when gigabit links were fancy and "cloud" meant weather. But its wisdom remains timeless. Especially if you've ever tried to troubleshoot a firewall rule chain in a rush.

20. Even now, you can find NetScreen boxes quietly guarding forgotten corners of the enterprise. They're in retail backrooms, remote substations, and "temporary" server closets that have been running since 2006. They're there, blinking softly, passing packets like retired martial artists who still spar at dawn just to stay sharp. Sure, they don't support modern ciphers. And yes, their GUIs look like a 2003 time capsule. But they haven't failed. They haven't cracked under load. And they still hold the line in places where IT budgets fear to tread. In those quiet corners, the **Scrolls of NetScreen live on**—like a well-worn manual, its pages curled, its contents battle-tested.

21. For students of Juniper Jitsu, understanding NetScreen is more than nostalgia—it's foundational. It teaches restraint. It teaches clarity. It teaches that not every problem needs 32 processors and AI analytics to solve. Sometimes, a 1U box with a good rule set and stable firmware is all you need. NetScreen reminds us to focus on purpose, not polish. On consistency, not flash. On building networks that don't need daily therapy to function. In an age of containerized chaos and YAML-induced panic attacks, there's something noble about that. So take a moment. Bow to the beige box.

22. NetScreen also taught the security world an important lesson about **feature discipline**. Not every box needs to do *everything*. It just needs to do its job well—and predictably. This became a guiding principle for SRX evolution, even as Juniper layered on more capability. They never strayed from the path of reliability, even when tempted by buzzword-laden trends. And for those of us who came up through the NetScreen era, it shaped how we approach architecture today. We don't just throw firewalls at problems—we apply logic, we use zones, and we log *everything*. We learned to respect uptime like it was a family heirloom. And that's a lesson worth keeping.

23. There are even whispers of a secret NetScreen cult—a few deeply loyal engineers who still run labs filled with restored 5GTs and SSGs. They speak fluent ScreenOS. They can subnet in hex. And they scoff at cloud-native frameworks that take 12 minutes to deploy and 9 minutes to fall over. These firewall shamans will tell you that the golden age wasn't flashy—it was *functional*. And they'll show you that, with enough tuning, a 15-year-old NetScreen can still block certain modern exploits. Is it ideal? No. Is it absurd? Absolutely. But that's part of the legacy. NetScreen wasn't just gear—it was a mindset.

24. In today's world of AI-driven everything and dashboards that require GPUs to render, it's easy to forget the elegance of NetScreen's design. But those who lived it… remember. They remember the smell of a new NetScreen-25 fresh from the box. They remember typing `get interface` like it was a nervous tic. They remember the sound of a VPN tunnel coming back up and knowing peace for another day. And they remember the ScreenOS CLI—not for its beauty, but for its consistency. It was the dojo floor on which many of us learned to fight. And no matter what comes next—whether it's cloud firewalls, AI-infused policy engines, or something coded in quantum Python—NetScreen will always be **where Juniper Jitsu began**.

25. So let us bow to the Scrolls of NetScreen—the foundational firewall force that shaped a generation of secure thinking. It was humble, fast, and predictable, like the ideal sensei. It taught us that security starts with structure, thrives on simplicity, and lives in stability. And it reminded us that flashy features fade, but strong fundamentals last forever. Whether you're defending a dusty server room or deploying SRX5800s in the cloud, the spirit of NetScreen flows through every packet you protect. It taught us not to fear the CLI, but to wield it. Not to chase every trend, but to master the principles. This was where the journey started. The first kata of Juniper Jitsu. And the foundation for every chapter that follows.

Chapter 2: SSG – Small-Scale Grandmaster

1. If NetScreen was the ancient scroll, then the **SSG series** was the portable pocketbook—a distilled, disciplined continuation of its philosophy with a few more muscles. SSG stood for **Secure Services Gateway**, which is marketing code for "This firewall does way more than its size suggests." These were the spiritual successors to the NetScreen-5GT and NetScreen-25, packing ScreenOS into refined form factors and injecting just enough horsepower to make security in tight spaces feel possible. Juniper built them for **small and medium businesses, retail outlets, remote branches**, and that one tech closet wedged behind the water heater. They weren't meant to dazzle—they were meant to *just work*, which they did… quietly, for years. With support for VPNs, dynamic routing, and zone-based firewalls, the SSGs carried the torch of simplicity and stability into a world increasingly obsessed with shiny dashboards. They were deploy-and-forget devices for many sysadmins—until the logs filled up or the remote config password got lost in an old binder. Still, they were champions of cost-efficiency and stealth. And in the right hands, they could deliver **black-belt-level packet blocking** with a 1U smile.

2. The SSG lineup was beautifully diverse—**SSG5, SSG20, SSG140, SSG320, and SSG550**, among others. From desktop-sized to rack-mountable, you had choices, and they all ran the same ScreenOS magic. The **SSG5 and SSG20** were the tiny titans—great for branches, home labs, or shoe closets doubling as server rooms. They had a few Ethernet ports, maybe a USB port, and just enough processing power to run VPN tunnels and simple policies without breaking a sweat. The **SSG140** added heft, more interfaces, and an attitude, while the **SSG320/SSG550** stepped into mid-sized enterprise territory. The higher-end models even supported **modular expansion cards**, making them feel just fancy enough to make Cisco users nervous. And yet, no matter the model, the configuration experience was consistent—**CLI-first, GUI-optional, and always unapologetically efficient**. You could go from box to baseline config in minutes, assuming you remembered to bring your serial cable and caffeine.

3. At a time when other vendors were overcomplicating firewalls, Juniper kept the SSG line laser-focused: **zone-based policy, rock-solid VPNs, and dependable routing**. ScreenOS offered **a consistent user experience** across all SSG devices, and that's not just marketing fluff —it mattered. You could learn on an SSG5 and manage an SSG550 with the exact same commands. From `set interface` to `get route`, the muscle memory translated cleanly, making SSGs a favorite in education, consulting, and MSP circles. They were the firewall equivalent of a trusted toolkit: basic, powerful, and unbreakable unless you really, really tried. They weren't flashy, and they didn't apologize for that. They knew their role—**secure the perimeter and do it without drama**. And when your CEO's laptop suddenly needed a VPN to the accounting server in Boise, the SSG had you covered.

4. VPN support in the SSG line was **top-notch**, thanks to NetScreen DNA flowing through their ports like encrypted espresso. You got **IPsec tunnels**, full crypto suite support, route-based and policy-based VPNs, and dynamic peer support for those with more ambition than patience. The SSG5 could hold its own with multiple concurrent tunnels, while the higher-end units could scale to full mesh if you gave them enough RAM and moral support. Configuring VPNs via CLI was faster than most GUI wizards, once you memorized the four magical scrolls: Phase 1, Phase 2, tunnel interface, and policy. VPNs were stable, lightweight, and didn't choke unless your broadband uplink turned into a potato. Remote access options were available too, and while not Juniper's strong suit, they got the job done. The only downside? Trying to explain IKE negotiations to someone using the web GUI. Still, **SSG VPNs were the quiet heroes of branch connectivity** for over a decade.

5. Logging on SSG devices was equal parts **minimalist and meaningful**. Logs were compact, focused, and written with the assumption that you were reading them on a 1999 CRT monitor. Each event gave you the essentials: source, destination, port, policy ID, and disposition. No unnecessary fluff, no analytics trying to guess the packet's personality. Logging destinations included the local file system (if you liked living dangerously), syslog servers (if you were a professional), and SNMP traps (if you hated yourself). Alerts could be emailed, assuming you were running an SMTP server and liked waking up at 3 a.m. If you were lucky, you built a simple SIEM around your SSG logs and started to feel feelings when the logs got too quiet. After all, **no logs doesn't mean no problems—it often means bigger ones**. In any case, the logs were there when you needed them—and out of the way when you didn't.

6. High availability in the SSG world was **less about elegance and more about commitment**. You could cluster two SSGs into an **active/passive HA pair** and keep your remote site breathing when storms hit the utility poles. The setup involved heartbeat interfaces, configuration syncs, and the occasional late-night console session where nothing worked until everything suddenly did. Failover was usually fast and sometimes even graceful. You could sync routes, NAT tables, VPN states, and more—but only if you RTFM'd every line of the manual and sacrificed a virgin cable tie to the networking gods. Still, **when it worked, it worked wonderfully**. And when it didn't? Well, that's why we had out-of-band management and several deeply personal recovery scripts. In short, SSGs *could* do HA—but you had to *really want it*.

7. One of the underrated SSG features was its support for **dynamic routing protocols**. Yes, you could run **RIP, OSPF, and BGP**—and the thing actually held its own. Routing in ScreenOS was refreshingly simple: define the protocol, the neighbors, and the area—done. You didn't need to write a thesis to understand the forwarding table. SSGs weren't going to replace your core router, but for small networks or WAN edge roles, they handled routing duties with stoic silence. OSPF peered without drama. BGP updated with dignity. Static routes still ruled the day, but if you needed protocols, the SSG delivered without complaining—or worse, rebooting. In fact, it was one of the few firewalls that didn't flinch when asked to do more than just block and log.

8. Interface flexibility was modest, but **surprisingly effective**. The smaller SSGs came with a handful of Fast Ethernet ports, while the 140s and up offered gigabit copper and fiber interfaces. You could configure interfaces as **Layer 3, Layer 2 (transparent), or Layer 2.5 (vaguely mystical)**. You could bind interfaces to zones, apply policies to those zones, and carve VLANs like a Thanksgiving turkey. Redundant Ethernet interfaces were supported for link failover, and with the right config, you could even run aggregate Ethernet (kind of). And yes, you could run PPPoE if you had to. We're sorry. We've all been there. But for most scenarios, **SSG interfaces were clean, flexible, and reliable**, like a good kung fu stance.

9. ScreenOS itself was still the **engine beneath the hood**, and SSGs inherited all the quirks, perks, and "oh dear, don't press that" moments from its NetScreen forebears. Firmware upgrades? Still a tense ceremony involving TFTP servers and backup configs. Configuration backups? A must. Running CLI commands felt like writing a firewall-themed haiku: `set interface ethernet0/0 zone untrust`, `set policy from trust to untrust any any permit log`. There were no namespaces, no multi-mode shells, and no JSON. And that was part of the charm. **You typed it, it worked, and you moved on with your life**. ScreenOS was stable, predictable, and deeply indifferent to your feelings. It just wanted to protect the packets and go back to blinking quietly.

10. If SSGs had a spirit animal, it would be **the stoic, overachieving underdog**. Never flashy, always functional. It didn't care if you gave it a fancy rack mount. It was happy in a dusty branch office, chugging away for 1,200 days without a reboot. It was often installed and forgotten—until someone needed to update a VPN and realized, with a gasp, that it *was still working flawlessly*. It survived reorgs, power outages, and IT turnover. It was the firewall equivalent of duct tape: not glamorous, but **essential to holding things together**. And while the world moved on to SRX, cloud-native firewalls, and container security, the SSG sat patiently… still scanning packets… still enforcing policy… still logging dropped pings from Gary's test server.

11. Perhaps the SSG's greatest achievement was **how well it aged**, like a vintage console cable or that one sysadmin hoodie that's somehow survived three companies. Even long after it was officially End-of-Life'd, many SSGs continued operating flawlessly in the field. They were used in roles from **VPN concentrators** to **policy firewalls**, to **"just make the internet work again" devices**. Some were even repurposed for labs, home networks, or as physical reminders that "they don't build 'em like this anymore." They had no fans, minimal power draw, and firmware so stable it could teach yoga. Sure, they lacked support for next-gen features like AppID or encrypted traffic inspection, but in many deployments, that didn't matter. They weren't about future-proofing. They were about *right-now reliability*. If there was a Hall of Fame for network gear that just refused to die, the SSG would be on the cover.

12. Troubleshooting on SSGs was **CLI-driven and deeply personal**. You didn't have dashboards. You had `get session`, `get route`, and the occasional desperate `exec debug`. You learned to read session tables like tea leaves—watching state transitions, timeout counters, and NAT mappings for signs of life (or death). Packet captures were crude but usable, especially once you figured out how to filter by interface and port. If you were really committed, you piped logs through grep and built mental timelines based on policy hits. There was no GUI "insight graph" to explain why DNS was failing—there was just you, the console, and the truth. And somehow, that made the victory sweeter. Because when you fixed it? You *earned* it. And then you backed up the config like a responsible adult.

13. SSGs taught thousands of admins the **importance of clarity in policy writing**. With no dynamic detection engines or app awareness, your rules had to be *tight*. "From trust to untrust, any any permit" was a rookie move. Veterans knew to specify source addresses, narrow destination ports, and apply logging sparingly—unless you wanted to fill your buffer faster than a YouTube video in 2008. Policies could be cloned and reordered, but you had to be deliberate. And the moment you saw "policy ID 14 matched" in a log, you better remember what policy 14 actually did. SSGs didn't make assumptions. They enforced what you typed. Which, in turn, taught you how to plan and document before clicking "commit." They were like firewall senseis: silent, strict, and very, very specific.

14. Performance on SSGs was **surprisingly robust**, considering the hardware looked like it ran on positive vibes and pocket lint. The smallest models could push a few megabits per second of full-duplex encrypted traffic, while the larger ones scaled into the hundreds. This wasn't SRX-level performance, but for most SMB and branch deployments, it was *plenty*. The custom ASICs continued to shine, offloading crypto tasks and session handling to keep the CPU calm and collected. Web surfing, VoIP, basic cloud apps—it all flowed through without complaint. Add too many UTM features, and yes, you might notice some strain. But for core firewall duties, the SSG was like a packet-processing monk: **efficient, focused, and unflappable**.

15. Licensing on SSGs was, blessedly, **simple and mostly optional**. The base feature set—firewall, NAT, VPN, routing—came unlocked. You could buy extra licenses for things like deep logging, dynamic routing scale, or UTM add-ons. But unlike modern platforms that require a license just to sneeze near a policy table, SSGs respected your time and budget. They didn't call home, didn't nag you, and didn't expire features in the middle of a crisis. You activated what you needed and forgot about it. This no-nonsense approach was part of what made them so popular. No one likes surprise firewalls. Especially not on a Friday. And the SSG? Never surprised anyone.

16. In the early days of **remote IT support**, the SSG became a secret weapon. Small enough to ship overnight, powerful enough to lock down a branch, and stable enough to survive long stretches without human interaction. You could configure one, test it in the lab, ship it to a site, and have someone plug it in with zero drama. Often, that person wasn't even in IT—they were just told, "Plug in cable A, then cable B." And the SSG? It picked up where you left off, as if no time had passed. It made remote provisioning feasible before the cloud made it fashionable. In a way, the SSG pioneered remote-first network thinking. Long before SD-WAN and zero-touch provisioning, there was the "I hope the receptionist plugged it in correctly" deployment model. And it worked.

17. Documentation for the SSG line was **dense, dry, and brilliant**. Juniper's ScreenOS guides were comprehensive and wonderfully old-school, filled with CLI examples, ASCII diagrams, and tables that went on for days. If you were willing to dig, you could learn everything—how to route, how to NAT, how to configure dual WAN failover while sipping bad coffee at 3 a.m. Unlike some vendors' cryptic guides, Juniper's ScreenOS docs assumed you were intelligent and stubborn—and rewarded both traits. The troubleshooting section alone was a gold mine. You learned about session timeouts, IKE phase mismatches, and how to politely argue with NAT rules. Over time, you began to trust the documentation almost as much as the device. And in this industry, that's saying something.

18. The GUI on SSGs… was a mixed bag. It technically existed. You could access it via HTTP or HTTPS, log in, and click around. For basic policy creation, interface assignments, and log review, it worked fine. But anything beyond that felt like trying to paint a bonsai tree with a roller brush. It lacked polish, sometimes lagged, and occasionally forgot what you were doing mid-session. Still, for users who weren't CLI-savvy, it provided a lifeline. And for others, it was the fastest way to verify whether someone else made changes without telling you. The GUI wasn't a masterpiece. But it was there. And it was often enough.

19. The SSG also marked **the beginning of Juniper's multi-role firewall concept**, long before it was cool. These boxes weren't just firewalls—they were routers, VPN gateways, access points (if you had the optional antenna!), and sometimes even DHCP servers. They were born to consolidate functionality in small spaces. One device to NAT them all, route them all, and log them into darkness. And while that all-in-one model has since evolved into cloud-managed edge platforms, the SSG did it first—and **did it surprisingly well**. It was a firewall with identity issues… and that identity was "everything your branch needs except snacks." For years, IT teams built entire network stacks around them. And many still stand today.

20. When the SRX series finally emerged, it didn't replace the SSG—it **inherited its mantle**. But the transition wasn't without bumps. SRX came with JunOS, a completely different OS that valued hierarchy, structure, and indentation over simplicity. SSG users were suddenly confronted with "commit confirm," rollback, and enough curly braces to start a JSON cult. Some adapted quickly. Others kept their SSGs running while quietly learning JunOS on the side like it was forbidden jutsu. And for a while, **both worlds existed in parallel**—ScreenOS for simplicity, JunOS for power. It was the great firewall fork of our time. And we all picked sides… at least until the hardware told us otherwise.

21. SSGs may not have supported deep inspection or app-awareness, but they forced us to **understand the fundamentals**. What's the source address? The destination port? Which policy is matching? Why is that NAT rule eating all my traffic like a hungry raccoon? These questions forged a generation of admins with real-world, hands-on skills. SSGs didn't hold your hand— they gave you the CLI, a blinking cursor, and the quiet confidence that the device would do *exactly what you told it to*. That meant the mistakes were yours. But so were the victories. It was firewalling without fluff, without fanfare, and without room for guessing. And that's what made it great.

22. Every SSG told a story. Some were shipped to oil rigs, others installed in mobile trailers or used to guard small-town libraries. They lived in harsh climates, under desks, and above ceiling tiles, usually plugged into unmanaged switches and labeled with Sharpie. And yet, they kept the internet flowing. They were the quiet companions of understaffed IT teams and first responders. They helped connect shelters, warehouses, and pop-up medical centers. They weren't flashy enough to make headlines, but they **made the mission possible**. And they did it all without asking for fanfare—or firmware upgrades. That's a legacy worth remembering.

23. Over time, SSGs have faded from the spotlight—but not from the racks. You'll still find them in legacy sites, lab environments, and situations where "if it ain't broke, don't replace it" is the law of the land. They're still out there, blinking confidently, guarding networks with honor and no illusions of grandeur. You won't see them on flashy analyst reports. They don't trend on Reddit. But they're **doing the work**—and doing it well. They serve as a reminder that good security isn't always about the latest AI. Sometimes, it's about **knowing your gear and trusting your config**. And the SSG always delivered both.

24. So what did the SSG teach us, in the grand scheme of Juniper Jitsu? That elegance and simplicity go hand in hand. That reliability is the best feature a firewall can offer. That every network, no matter how small, deserves structure, visibility, and zone-based kung fu. And that sometimes, a humble, feature-light box with four ports and a stubborn CLI can defend your network *better* than gear with blinking LEDs and marketing buzzwords. SSG was the quiet master. The one who trained you without saying much. And when you finally moved on to SRX or beyond, it bowed quietly and let you go.

25. Thus ends the tale of the **Small-Scale Grandmaster** — a firewall forged from legacy wisdom, powered by stoic firmware, and remembered fondly by those who typed `set int eth0/0 zone untrust` a thousand times. If NetScreen was the scroll that began your journey, the SSG was your *first real training partner*. It taught you to think like a firewall, to write policies with intention, and to troubleshoot like a legend. It's gone from the shelves, but not from our hearts — or our subnets. And now, as we close this chapter and prepare to meet the **ISG — the Industrial Strength Grappler** — remember: Every ninja starts small. Every master starts with a blinking box.

Chapter 3: ISG Series – Industrial Strength Grapple

1. If NetScreen was the scroll and SSG was the apprentice, then **ISG — the Integrated Security Gateway** — was the full-contact security dojo built from reinforced chassis and caffeinated ASICs. Designed for large enterprises, service providers, and data centers that feared neither uptime demands nor excessive fan noise, the ISG series was Juniper's way of saying, "Here's your firewall, router, VPN concentrator, IPS platform, and rack heater — all in one." These were not plug-and-play devices for your cousin's dental office. These were industrial-grade packet-slicing platforms that *meant business*. Big throughput, redundant power, modular interfaces, and the soul of a samurai in a 3U form factor. You didn't deploy an ISG casually. You **installed** it like a server, assigned it a guardian role, and hoped your power budget could handle it. They ran ScreenOS, but wore it like armor — adding features, performance, and ports with every blade you slid into them. Simply put: **ISG was NetScreen's final form**.

2. The lineup was led by two core models: the **ISG1000** and the **ISG2000**. The ISG1000 was powerful, modular, and fully capable of defending a medium-to-large enterprise's perimeter. But the **ISG2000?** That thing was a fortress with Ethernet ports. It supported **two IDP security modules**, multiple interface cards, redundant fans, and the airflow of a wind tunnel. You could build custom configurations for firewalling, deep packet inspection, VPN concentration, and even transparent inline IDS/IPS functionality. There were SFP slots, copper ports, fiber interfaces, and more expansion options than a conspiracy theory subreddit. For once, the phrase "next-gen" actually made sense—it was firewall, IDS, and routing muscle, all working under one hood. And despite all that capability, it still booted faster than most laptops. ISG wasn't just a box—it was **a statement**.

3. What made ISG truly deadly in the art of Juniper Jitsu was its **support for IDP security modules**. These were **add-in blades** that gave the ISG the ability to go beyond basic port-based filtering into **true intrusion detection and prevention**. We're talking signature-based inspection, anomaly detection, TCP reassembly, protocol validation—the whole nine gigabits. With IDP blades installed, the ISG became a **serious contender** in the IDS/IPS space. No longer just a firewall, it now had eyes deep into layer 7, and it could **actively block** known threats with precision. The policies could be layered: firewall policy, IDP policy, VPN policy—all marching in elegant lockstep. And thanks to the modularity, you could scale performance by adding SPU modules or upgrading memory—**a rare treat in fixed appliance firewalls**. If your threats scaled, ISG scaled with you.

4. The routing capabilities of the ISG series were no joke, either. These beasts weren't just packet-blockers—they could act as **core network routers**. Full support for **RIP, OSPF, BGP**, static routes, policy-based routing, and VRRP made them ideal for edge deployments and multi-homed environments. Want to route between MPLS links, metro Ethernet, and a VPN? ISG shrugged and said, "Sure, but bring coffee." Route redistribution worked cleanly, and ScreenOS allowed for route filtering and tweaking without the emotional breakdown common in other platforms. You could even run the ISG in **transparent mode**, bridging networks with full inspection without changing the underlying topology. It was like a ninja walking through walls— **still enforcing policies, still unseen**. This wasn't just a firewall. It was **a high-speed, zone-based router that happened to carry throwing stars**.

5. VPN on ISG was next-level, with **hardware acceleration baked in** for bulk crypto operations. Thousands of tunnels? No problem. ISG handled them like meditation—calm, efficient, and always present. IPsec? Sure. GRE over IPsec? Absolutely. Dynamic VPNs with IKE Phase 1 and 2 options so flexible they made most engineers slightly uncomfortable? Of course. Whether you were doing hub-and-spoke, full mesh, or some twisted VPN hairball you inherited from a merger, ISG could handle it. With dual crypto engines, you could scale without burning CPU. This was *firewall-fu with a VPN twist*. And you better believe your competitors noticed when you turned on anti-replay and tunnel failover without packet loss.

6. Policies on the ISG weren't just scalable—they were **a firewall manifesto**. You could write thousands of rules, layer them by zone, apply application services, set scheduling, and log at multiple levels. Match by interface, user, group, time of day, IP, and service. Need to allow HTTPS outbound during business hours but only for one subnet and only if it's not Friday? Done. And with policy-based routing tied to those same rules, you could steer traffic as a

response to behavior, not just configuration. ISG was policy-first security before it was trendy. Each rule was a tiny contract between trust zones. And once written, it enforced those rules like a digital sensei with no tolerance for nonsense.

7. Logging and monitoring were critical in ISG deployments—and ScreenOS delivered. Logs could be pushed to **syslog, SNMP, NetScreen Security Manager (NSM)**, or directly viewed from the CLI. Each log entry gave source, destination, port, interface, zone, policy hit, and session state. No fluff, just facts. Real-time log streaming meant your SOC could react to events as they unfolded—not after the damage was done. You could define **custom logging thresholds**, suppress noisy events, and even route log severity levels to different systems. That meant you could track critical drops in one place and send successful VPN handshakes to another. Combined with **IDP alerts**, the ISG became an all-seeing sentry—**always watching, never overwhelmed**.

8. High availability was practically a religion in the ISG world. You had **active/passive clustering**, full configuration and session synchronization, and support for multiple heartbeat paths. Failovers could happen seamlessly, with full VPN and session retention. Redundant power supplies kept the box humming through brownouts. And the fans? Loud enough to remind you of their importance. Many ISGs ran in mission-critical environments with **five nines uptime**, quietly doing their job while lesser appliances collapsed under load or misconfigured BGP. When paired with NSM, failover events could be logged, alerted, and analyzed to prevent future downtime. HA in ISG wasn't a checkbox—it was **an operational philosophy**.

9. NSM—**NetScreen Security Manager**—was the preferred management platform for larger ISG deployments. It allowed you to push policy changes, manage firmware, view real-time logs, and enforce standards across dozens (or hundreds) of firewalls. Sure, the interface looked like it was designed by someone who'd never used a mouse. But it was powerful, scalable, and **kept big networks in check**. Through NSM, the ISG series could operate as part of a larger, orchestrated security fabric. It meant **centralized policy management**, audit logging, change tracking, and role-based access controls. For large enterprises, it was a godsend. For small shops… well, you probably just stuck to CLI.

10. One of the ISG's unique features was **deep integration with Juniper's early IDP engines**, allowing for inline IPS with full packet inspection. You could build custom signatures, apply traffic normalization, and define actions ranging from log-only to drop-and-sanitize. This meant **proactive defense** against worms, port scans, buffer overflow attempts, and even certain types of application abuse. The ISG didn't just watch—it intervened. You could throttle, block, or shun repeat offenders. And the best part? It did all this **without needing to redirect traffic to an external box**. With the right IDP module and policy tuning, your firewall became a **full-spectrum threat prevention system**. And your attackers? They became confused, frustrated, and blocked.

11. The ISG wasn't just about power—it was about **purpose-built performance**. Every slot, screw, and silicon slice was designed for serious workloads. You didn't deploy an ISG to "test things out." You deployed it when uptime mattered, when you needed logs that made sense, and when **your boss's boss's VPN** depended on zero drama. Performance scaled based on how many modules you installed and what services were enabled. With full IDP, heavy VPN load, and a long policy list, the ISG still punched through gigabits like they were soft tofu. But when you ran it lean, it was even faster—**a packet-processing ninja stripped for speed**. Its modularity gave you the choice. And that, more than anything, made ISG a rare gem in the rigid world of pre-cloud appliances.

12. The physical design of the ISG screamed "I have **opinions about uptime**." Dual power supplies, modular interface cards, replaceable fans, and front-facing ports for ease of cable zen. It even had **field-replaceable components**, which meant fewer "forklift upgrades" and more "just swap the bad blade and carry on." The airflow was deliberate and forceful, like it was daring the dust to try anything. Rack rails were standard, and yes—if you dropped it, **it would probably survive better than your foot**. You didn't just rack an ISG—you *ceremonially installed* it. And once installed, it occupied its space like a digital shrine to packet discipline. Servers came and went, switches aged and died—but the ISG remained.

13. Security zones were the ISG's **spiritual battlefield**, and every traffic flow was a duel judged by policy. Just like in its SSG and NetScreen ancestors, traffic rules were written between zones, not interfaces—offering abstraction, clarity, and **a deeply satisfying structure**. You could create as many custom zones as needed: WAN, DMZ, VPN, Partners, Guest, Finance, that one server you don't trust anymore—whatever made sense. Then you wrote explicit policies between those zones with actions: permit, deny, tunnel, or tarpit. And like any true sensei, the ISG followed your instructions *exactly*. If traffic flowed where it shouldn't, it was because **you told it to**—intentionally or otherwise. This strictness didn't just reduce errors—it **taught respect for policy logic**. Admins who trained on ISG rarely made the same mistake twice.

14. Troubleshooting on ISG was an **educational experience**—equal parts brutal honesty and enlightenment. You had real-time session tables, deep logging, verbose debug modes, and even packet captures that didn't require an external span port. Tools like `get session`, `get counter`, and `exec ping` were your lifelines, and if all else failed, there was always `debug flow basic`—the firewall equivalent of staring into the abyss. ISG wouldn't hide the truth from you. If your config was broken, it told you. If traffic was blocked, it logged exactly which policy slammed the door. It wasn't hand-holding—but it was *empowering*. **You fixed it. You learned. You emerged stronger.** ISG didn't just pass traffic—it forged network ninjas in fire and logs.

15. The ISG supported **VLAN tagging**, sub-interfaces, trunking, and even Layer 2 transparent mode for more advanced segmentation. You could place multiple VLANs on a single physical interface and assign each to a different zone. Want to run a guest subnet, a finance VLAN, and a dev lab through one uplink? Go ahead. Each gets its own security policy, NAT rules, and logging. Transparent mode let you insert the ISG into a live network without disrupting IP schemes—a stealthy move when you needed **inline IPS without topological trauma**. You could even NAT in bridge mode, which felt like breaking the laws of networking physics. It wasn't always pretty, but it was effective. And once again, **the flexibility rewarded the prepared**.

16. On the topic of NAT, ISG offered a **full buffet of translation options**. Source NAT, destination NAT, static NAT, and everything in between—including that weird "many-to-one with round-robin fallback" thing you did once in 2011 and still regret. It supported PAT, port forwarding, and one-to-one mapping across interfaces and zones. NAT policies could be written cleanly, with matching security rules and logging. And when NAT broke things—as it inevitably does—the ISG gave you the tools to *see* it. Session tables, flow debugs, and NAT hit counters made the invisible visible. Yes, NAT was sometimes painful. But at least with ISG, it was **pain with visibility**.

17. User-based access was limited in ISG compared to modern systems, but it still **offered local users, LDAP/RADIUS integration**, and policy enforcement by user group. This was useful for remote VPN access or enforcing limited admin controls. You couldn't do full-blown identity-based firewalling, but you could say things like "Only users in Group X can access Subnet Y." For the time, this was cutting-edge. And while today's tools have made identity-aware policies more granular, the ISG **paved the way** by proving they were useful at all. It made firewalls smarter. And it made admins ask better questions.

18. Firmware upgrades on ISG were always an **event**. You had to stage the image, verify compatibility, schedule downtime (or not), and **hold your breath during the reboot**. But the process was predictable, well-documented, and rarely fatal. ISG didn't break lightly. And rollback was always an option—just in case your "minor update" turned into a major Friday evening regret. Most admins kept a known-good version handy, just in case. Like any powerful ninja, the ISG respected caution. And if you gave it a stable release and the right incantations? It ran **forever**.

19. From a deployment perspective, ISG boxes were **strategic assets**, not tactical band-aids. You didn't buy one unless you had a plan—and a rack. They anchored the edge of datacenters, sat between core switches and external networks, and defended zones like digital paladins. They replaced multiple point solutions: firewall, VPN concentrator, IPS, and sometimes router. They were a **Swiss Army firewall**, but made of titanium. And if you configured them well, they required **almost no attention**—just check the logs, rotate the keys, and update the firmware every now and then (with prayer). They weren't flashy—but they were **unshakable**.

20. The ISG era gave birth to **some of the most battle-hardened network admins in existence**. Working with ISG meant you knew your protocols, you wrote clean policies, and you didn't panic during a failover. You understood zone logic, NAT flow, VPN negotiation, and how to read a log line like it owed you money. If you cut your teeth on ISG, you could walk into any firewall job and ask, "CLI or GUI?" with a smirk. It trained generations of engineers to think modularly, act cautiously, and plan like network samurai. It was **more than a firewall**—it was a dojo. And it showed.

21. In many deployments, ISG gear **outlived the network it was defending**. Servers got virtualized, switches got replaced, and apps moved to the cloud—but the ISG? Still there. Still inspecting. Still logging. It was common to find ISG boxes running with over 1,000 days of uptime, blinking proudly as if to say, "I've seen things. I've dropped things. I'm still here." They weren't meant to be immortal, but no one told them that. And when it finally came time to decommission them? Admins *hesitated*. Because some devices earn your respect.

22. Even today, the legacy of ISG lives on in modern SRX appliances. The idea of modular security, inline inspection, and highly customizable policy logic? Straight from the ISG's playbook. Concepts like **zones, policy-based VPN, dynamic routing support, and HA clustering** all evolved directly from the ISG lineage. It wasn't just a firewall—it was a **blueprint for how Juniper Jitsu would scale**. The SRX series added new tricks: AppSecure, JunOS, SDN support—but the core? That was ISG's DNA. And you can feel it every time you write a clean, logical, zone-based policy.

23. The ISG was never flashy—but it was **legendary**. It was the firewall you trusted when everything else was questionable. The one you knew would hold the line when the power flickered, when the VPNs surged, when the scans started. It didn't advertise its strength. It didn't need marketing slides. It just *worked*. Day after day, packet after packet. And for a generation of security pros, that's all it needed to do.

24. So as you browse sleek modern dashboards, push policies via APIs, and inspect TLS 1.3 payloads with cloud-native sensors, **take a moment**. Remember the ISG. The box that taught you structure. The firewall that punished bad configs—but only to make you stronger. The quiet beast in the rack that didn't reboot for three years. Because while technology evolves, the principles don't. **Discipline. Visibility. Control. Consistency.** That's the ISG code. And it still holds.

25. Thus concludes the tale of the **Industrial Strength Grappler**—a true master of Juniper Jitsu. It brought modularity, muscle, and mastery to the firewall form. It wasn't cute. It wasn't quiet. But it *was* reliable, respected, and still fondly remembered in IT war stories. Whether you deployed one in a bank, a campus, or a bunker, you knew the ISG would never flinch. And that's what made it special. The next time someone praises their new firewall's uptime, smile quietly and think: "My ISG did that *before breakfast*."Chapter 4: IDP Series – The First True Senseis of Detection

Chapter 4: IDP Series – The First True Senseis of Detection

1. Before NGFWs made the term "deep inspection" sound like a spa treatment, there was Juniper's **IDP series**—the **Intrusion Detection and Prevention** devices that stared into packet payloads and saw through lies. While ISG and SSG focused on policy enforcement, the IDP appliances were **specialists**—built solely to detect and prevent malicious activity at a granular, signature-driven level. They were not firewalls, but they worked alongside them like the quiet sensei in the corner, watching every move with surgical precision. Born from the spirit of **NetScreen and Juniper's acquisition of OneSecure**, the IDP line marked Juniper's first step into full-on Layer 7 security. These were boxes that didn't just block bad ports—they knew the difference between a normal HTTP GET and one trying to smuggle malware in a cookie. And while they lacked the universal glamour of their firewall cousins, they *earned respect* from anyone who configured one, tuned its policies, and saw it catch something no one else could. This was **detection done right**, long before it became a buzzword.

2. The IDP lineup included models like the IDP 50, 200, 600, 800, 8200, and 8200EX—ranging from modest branch devices to datacenter monsters capable of seeing every sneeze across a continent's worth of traffic. The IDP 50 was the runt of the litter, small but scrappy. The IDP 800 and 600 handled midsize workloads, while the 8200 and 8200EX were the equivalent of wire-speed exorcists. Each model came with a dedicated CPU, a serious amount of RAM (for its time), and ASIC support for signature inspection and packet normalization. They were deployed inline, in tap mode, or as Layer 2 bridges, depending on the mood of the network and your appetite for risk. These appliances didn't mess around. They scanned traffic as it passed, compared it against signature databases, and made decisions in real time—like bouncers with a blacklist and perfect recall. And if they weren't sure, they logged it, alerted it, and gave you enough data to make your own ninja call.

3. The IDP engine at the core of these devices was a signature-based marvel—not just matching strings, but parsing protocols and behaviors to look for suspicious patterns. You had categories like malware, trojans, exploits, spyware, reconnaissance, evasion techniques, and policy violations. Each category contained hundreds (eventually thousands) of attack signatures—regularly updated by Juniper's security team and fed to devices via a sacred ritual involving web updates and schedule windows. Rules could be applied with different severities and responses: log only, drop packet, drop session, close client, close server, quarantine. The appliance didn't just alert you—it could act, stopping threats at the first sign of trouble. You could also define custom signatures, which either made you feel like a cyber wizard or a regex victim, depending on the day. But when you nailed one? Chef's kiss. The IDP engine was your microscope, your guard dog, and your early warning system.

4. Configuration and management were handled via IDP Device Manager (IDP DM) or the broader NSM (NetScreen Security Manager) platform. And yes—there was a GUI, albeit one that looked like it was built on a dare in Java Swing. You could browse rules, update signatures, build policies, and deploy them to multiple devices. The learning curve was real, especially for those used to CLI-only firewalls. But the payoff was massive. Once you understood how the engine worked—predefined rulebases, action types, severity levels—you could deploy proactive defenses against entire classes of attacks. Need to block known command-and-control (C2) channels? There's a rule for that. Want to detect potential SQL injection attempts? One click, and done. It wasn't as sleek as modern UIs, but it worked. And if you ever used IDP DM to successfully block a buffer overflow? You never forgot it.

5. IDP appliances operated in three primary modes: inline, tap (mirror), and transparent. Inline was full-on samurai mode—packets passed through the device and could be dropped on the spot. Tap mode allowed passive detection without disruption, perfect for SOCs who needed to monitor first and break things later. Transparent mode sat like a ghost on the wire, forwarding traffic while applying Layer 2 magic and detection logic. Each mode had its trade-offs: inline gave control, tap gave visibility, and transparent gave stealth. And deploying them was relatively painless—once you read the 400-page deployment guide. Many organizations started in tap mode to "see what's out there," then gradually moved to inline once they saw the flood of poorly behaved packets their users had normalized. This was training wheels for visibility—and many teams learned to ride fast.

6. The real magic of the IDP series came from its protocol decoders—specialized engines that understood the actual structure of application protocols like HTTP, FTP, SMTP, DNS, and more. These weren't just pattern matchers; they parsed payloads like linguistic professors with paranoia issues. That meant they could detect malformed requests, suspicious headers, or unexpected sequences that indicated attempts at evasion or exploitation. The decoders were deeply contextual, able to tell the difference between a poorly written script and an actual attack. And because they worked alongside signatures, you got layered detection—catching both known threats and shady behavior. This was real Layer 7 inspection, before anyone slapped "next-gen" on their brochure. And once you tuned it properly? The IDP could sniff out evil like a truffle pig in a data center.

7. Logging and alerting in the IDP series were as detailed as you dared to enable. Events could be filtered by severity, protocol, source/destination, rule match, and even the stage of the connection where detection occurred. You could log to syslog, SNMP traps, IDP DM, NSM, or even export in XML for the sad soul building a custom SIEM parser. The alerts were verbose, contextual, and occasionally hilarious ("This session was closed because it made us uncomfortable"). You could configure thresholds to prevent alert storms, create suppression lists for known noisy applications, and even generate reports that made management think you had magical foresight. And if you ever used the real-time alert viewer during a live attack, it was like watching a cyber thriller unfold in command-line cinema. Red alerts. Flow direction arrows. Packets that screamed, "Block me, sensei!"

8. Signature updates were both essential and occasionally emotionally loaded. Juniper's STRIKE team (Security Threat Response, Intelligence, Knowledge, and Education—yes, they tried) delivered updates that included new signatures, updated threat descriptions, and the occasional fix for a rule that matched everything. You could schedule updates, manually import them, or build custom deployments in NSM. Each signature came with a CVE reference (when applicable), a description of the exploit, and guidance on action types. This gave security teams both tactical and strategic value: immediate protection and long-term context. When updates went smoothly, they were a thing of beauty. When they broke something? Well, that's why you had a rollback plan and a dev copy of the policy. Because even ninja scrolls need proofreading.

9. Performance on the IDP series was heavily dependent on proper tuning. Out of the box, the full rulebase could crush your throughput faster than a misconfigured IDS in a 10G environment. But once you filtered out unnecessary rules, prioritized signatures by relevance, and tuned thresholds for alerting, the system ran beautifully. Smart deployments used policy layering, custom rule groups, and traffic-specific tuning to get the most out of each box. And Juniper gave you the tools—flow charts, hit counters, drop logs—to adjust accordingly. This wasn't set-it-and-forget-it security. It was adaptive defense that rewarded those willing to learn. And once you hit that sweet spot between detection fidelity and performance? Chef's kiss again.

10. In the grand history of Juniper Jitsu, the IDP series holds a unique title: the first dedicated sensei of network behavior. It didn't replace firewalls. It enhanced them. It worked in harmony with SSG, ISG, and later SRX devices—either inline or side-by-side, always alert, always observing. And in doing so, it brought awareness to layers of the network that traditional firewalls never touched. It turned "what port is that?" into "why is this traffic pretending to be HTTPS while delivering shellcode?" It trained analysts to ask better questions, and gave them the tools to find answers. It wasn't glamorous. It wasn't trendy. But it was the first real move toward intelligent packet judgment. And for that, it deserves our respect.

11. One of the key superpowers of the IDP series was its **evasion technique detection**—because attackers rarely knock politely when breaking in. The IDP didn't just look for payloads; it looked for tricks. Fragmented packets? Flagged. TCP segmentation with reordered payloads? Noticed. Unicode double encoding to bypass filters? Caught red-handed. The device understood that the best attacks weren't always about raw exploitation—they were about **confusion and misdirection**. By reassembling streams, validating protocol compliance, and analyzing patterns, the IDP saw through the smoke. It even detected timing-based evasion attempts, because nothing says "I'm guilty" like a TCP handshake that takes longer than your lunch break. This kind of insight wasn't just helpful—it was **game-changing** for analysts who previously blamed "the internet being weird."

12. In environments where **regulatory compliance** mattered, IDP appliances became the best friend of every overworked auditor. HIPAA? PCI-DSS? SOX? Pick your acronym. The IDP's logs, reports, and granular control made it easier to demonstrate that you weren't just protecting data—you were **watching it with laser-guided policy enforcement**. You could create rules for data leakage, track usage patterns, and detect unauthorized protocols in places they had no business being (we're looking at you, Telnet on port 80). Alert thresholds, event correlation, and real-time logging offered **proof of vigilance** that regulators loved and attackers hated. Sure, it wouldn't make your compliance meetings more exciting—but it would make them shorter. And in corporate security, that's practically a party.

13. Some IDP deployments went **fully inline with auto-blocking enabled**, turning the appliance into a one-box judge, jury, and packet executioner. For brave souls (or reckless optimists), this mode delivered maximum protection—instantaneous action on detection, and zero tolerance for protocol weirdness. For cautious admins, this mode came with a side of Rolaids. When properly tuned, inline blocking worked beautifully. But if your rule tuning was sloppy or you accidentally applied the "drop all invalid HTTP" policy to your internal DevOps tools… well, *suddenly nothing worked and everyone blamed DNS*. That's why most IDP admins started in detection-only mode, reviewed logs, then moved incrementally toward enforcement. Because **a wise ninja always tests their blade before swinging**.

14. Speaking of wisdom, Juniper's IDP documentation was a **mixed scroll** of enlightenment and cryptic poetry. Some sections were crystal clear, with flow diagrams, rule examples, and "here's why this matters" sidebars. Other sections? Let's just say they assumed you already achieved firewall enlightenment and could speak fluent SNMP hex dumps. Fortunately, the IDP community stepped in—forums, user groups, and third-party guides filled the gaps with practical, field-tested advice. Best practices were shared like ancient kung fu secrets: don't enable everything, prioritize by environment, and always backup before deploying a new signature pack. And if the official documentation didn't help? Well, that's what `tail -f` and espresso were for.

15. Integration with firewalls was seamless but optional. The IDP could live beside your **ISG, SSG, or SRX,** or it could sit on its own tap port like a philosophical monk watching the packets flow by. Inline deployments were more powerful, but required architectural courage. Out-of-band deployments offered **visibility without impact**, ideal for organizations that needed to observe first and act later. Either way, IDP data was **gold dust** to the security team. It enriched alerts, added behavioral context, and helped SOC analysts draw conclusions faster. Even when the IDP wasn't blocking, it was enabling **smarter defense** by feeding intelligence into other systems. It was like having a scout that never slept—and never sugarcoated its findings.

16. The **update cadence** for signatures was frequent and focused—Juniper released new definitions based on emerging threats, zero-days, and vulnerability disclosures. STRIKE updates weren't flashy, but they were **reliable and meaningful**, always accompanied by release notes and affected CVEs. Signature categories could be toggled on or off, allowing organizations to tailor detection to their industry (because your finance department probably doesn't need aggressive SIP inspection). The update system was lightweight and worked via CLI or GUI. And for truly custom environments, you could even write your own signatures to detect internal policy violations, command-line tools in the wild, or unauthorized applications. This wasn't just network security—it was **network behavioral training**.

17. Over time, many IDP appliances were pulled into **distributed security architectures**, working in tandem with SIEMs, firewalls, endpoint agents, and honeypots. They served as central detection nodes—early-warning systems that shouted loudest when something truly dangerous was on the move. In red team/blue team exercises, the IDP often played the role of **silent whistleblower**, catching exfil attempts and lateral scans long before other systems raised a peep. They weren't designed to replace full SIEMs or endpoint protection. They were **laser-focused on the network layer**, and that's what made them so valuable. They didn't try to be everything. They just tried to be **right**.

18. One of the lesser-known but deeply appreciated features was the **Ability to Correlate Events Over Time**. The IDP engine could track session history, detect recurring patterns, and even *learn* from certain behaviors to reduce false positives. You could build logic trees like, "If this host scans five ports, then attempts an FTP connection, flag it as a reconnaissance sequence." This was IDS as a **living policy framework**, not just a signature graveyard. These correlation features weren't AI—but they were **smart enough to be useful without a PhD**. And in a world full of alert fatigue, this feature helped cut through the noise like a katana through compliance memos.

19. The **real-world impact** of IDP deployments was often subtle but profound. You didn't always notice when it blocked a C2 callback or quietly shut down a malformed packet storm. But you *did* notice when attacks slowed, when incident tickets dropped, and when late-night calls became less frequent. The IDP brought balance. It reduced reliance on human detection. It empowered teams to focus on the weird and novel instead of the obvious and repetitive. It was the difference between surviving attacks and **anticipating them**. And for many teams, it was the first time they truly *felt secure*.

20. And yes—sometimes the IDP series made mistakes. False positives happened. Debug sessions got wild. Tuning a rule set after a major signature update could make even experienced admins question their life choices. But the platform *always gave you tools to fix it*. Nothing was hidden. Every packet inspected, every rule matched, every drop or alert—**it was all visible and controllable**. IDP was never about guessing. It was about truth. Even when that truth was, "You accidentally blocked HR from their email again."

21. In a world that was still warming up to the idea of deep packet inspection, the IDP series was ahead of its time. It was not content to just log the outer shell of a packet. It wanted to **understand the soul of the traffic**—its origin, purpose, behavior, and eventual consequences. While other appliances counted packets, the IDP was analyzing **intent**. That kind of thinking laid the groundwork for everything we now call "next-gen" or "behavioral" security. The IDP didn't need a hype man. It just needed **a good policy and a reliable power supply**.

22. As threats grew more sophisticated and encrypted traffic rose, the IDP line began its graceful exit, gradually merging into newer platforms. Many of its capabilities were absorbed into **SRX with AppSecure**, and its mindset continues in **Sky ATP and Juniper's modern detection stack**. But old-school IDP appliances? They still show up in dusty racks, quietly running, still logging, still catching things no one expected. Like forgotten monks in mountaintop temples, they don't brag. They don't break. And they never stop watching.

23. If you ever worked on an IDP, you became **a better defender**. You learned what real network behavior looked like. You stopped thinking in ports and started thinking in *payloads*. You learned to trust patterns, verify anomalies, and never assume silence meant safety. You read logs like tea leaves. You treated alerts with skepticism, respect, and sometimes outright horror. And when the IDP lit up at 2 a.m., you *paid attention*. Because it wasn't prone to drama. If it screamed, something was on fire.

24. So let us honor the **IDP Series**—the first senseis of detection, the eagle-eyed guardians, the protocol-whispering legends of Layer 7. They weren't glamorous. They weren't simple. But they were **right** more often than they were wrong. And in this industry, that's worth more than all the AI dashboards and blockchain compliance tools in the world. These boxes stood guard. They taught. They logged. And they warned us before we knew we needed warning.

25. Thus concludes the scroll of the IDP Series. They saw deeper. They judged smarter. And they made us better at what we do. Their legacy lives on in every intrusion policy, every behavioral signature, and every analyst who once said, "Oh wow, it actually caught that." Onward, to **Chapter 5 – IDP-50: Tiny Box, Big Punchlines**, where we meet the smallest sensor in the series—small in form, *mighty in sass*.

Chapter 5: IDP-50 – Tiny Box, Big Punchlines

1. In the grand dojo of intrusion detection, the **IDP-50** was the student who looked like he wandered in by mistake—until he promptly dismantled a threat using nothing but timing, minimal specs, and righteous signature packs. Designed for **small offices, remote branches, and lab environments**, the IDP-50 was Juniper's bite-sized brawler in the world of intrusion prevention. You could hold it in one hand and still feel its packet-sensing presence humming like a katana in standby mode. This was **not** a high-performance appliance—it was a **precise**, **deliberate**, and **affordable** ninja sent to quietly observe, report, and intervene when needed. It ran the same IDP engine as its bigger siblings, which meant it had all the brains—just in a much smaller, more caffeinated body. If it missed a threat, it wasn't because it didn't know—it was probably just busy with a thousand other packets at the same time. But when tuned right and placed carefully in the network, the IDP-50 punched **well above its weight class**. And let's be honest: it was adorable. A pocket protector with payload paranoia.

2. From a hardware perspective, the IDP-50 was a **marvel of minimalist design**. It came with **a few Ethernet ports**, modest RAM, and a compact form factor that looked more like a router you'd find in a cereal box than an actual intrusion prevention system. It didn't have a fancy display, hot-swappable anything, or glowing LED unicorns. What it had was **pure intent**. It booted fast, ran quiet, and sipped power like a Zen monk in an energy drink factory. You could slide it onto a bookshelf, tuck it behind a monitor, or even Velcro it to the underside of a desk (don't ask). Its footprint was small, but its logs? **Voluminous**. This was a surveillance device disguised as a shoebox. And it thrived in networks where **space was tight and threats were real**.

3. The IDP-50 supported **inline and tap modes**, just like its larger siblings, allowing it to be deployed passively or with teeth. Most admins started with **tap mode**, using it to sniff traffic and raise alerts like a tiny conspiracy theorist with a Wireshark addiction. It could monitor web browsing, detect scanning behavior, and flag protocol anomalies—all without dropping a packet. Inline mode required more planning but gave you **true mitigation capability**. Did someone plug in a malware-ridden thumb drive and start spewing SMB exploits like a digital sprinkler? The IDP-50 saw it. Blocked it. Logged it. Probably judged it. It wasn't fast, but it was **thorough**. And in a quiet office, that's exactly what you needed.

4. Signature updates for the IDP-50 were the **same glorious scrolls of wisdom** used by the 8200EX—albeit with a few performance caveats. Yes, you could load the full signature pack, but doing so was like asking a hamster to pull a shopping cart uphill in July. The smart move was **selective signature deployment**: pick the ones that mattered, prune the ones that didn't, and always monitor CPU load like it owed you money. You could filter by category (exploits, policy violations, reconnaissance), prioritize based on traffic profile, and disable anything you weren't actively worried about (RIP protocol, anyone?). It was all about balance. In return, the IDP-50 gave you **lightning-fast alerts** for the rules it could handle and respectfully ignored the ones it couldn't. A lesson in humility, really.

5. Logging on the IDP-50 was **beautiful in its brutal honesty**. If something looked even remotely suspicious, it logged it. If you so much as sneezed on port 445, it had a timestamped entry ready to go. Logs could be streamed to NSM, sent to syslog, or even exported manually via the GUI—if you had the patience and weren't afraid of Java applets. Each log entry included source, destination, attack category, action taken, and the ever-reassuring message: *"Session closed: suspicious activity detected."* Was it overkill? Sometimes. But better too loud than too late. And if you were running a small SOC or troubleshooting a sketchy user, the IDP-50's logs were like reading a **digital diary of mischief and mayhem**.

6. For organizations with multiple small sites, the IDP-50 offered something rare: **standardized, scalable intrusion detection for the edge**. You could deploy them across retail stores, branch offices, or remote teams without needing a rack, HVAC, or full-time IT ninja on staff. Centralized management via NSM meant you could push updates, tune policies, and **monitor dozens of devices from a single control plane**. It wasn't just convenience—it was **force multiplication**. Now your entire organization had eyes in places it never did before. Even if the nearest IT staffer was two time zones away and allergic to CLI.

7. Despite its size, the IDP-50 could still run **custom signatures**, which meant you could turn it into a specialist device. Want to catch employees using Tor at a donut shop? Write a rule. Need to detect unauthorized FTP uploads from Gary in Accounting again? Write a rule. As long as you respected the hardware limits, the IDP-50 didn't care how niche your policies were—it just wanted to **sniff packets and tell the truth**. This level of flexibility made it a favorite for **compliance teams and tinfoil-hat admins alike**. It was your little, loyal watchdog with a keen nose for nonsense.

8. The IDP-50 wasn't built for speed—it was built for **intentional inspection**. If you pushed too much traffic through it, it would protest. If you overloaded it with rules, it would sigh and start dropping sessions. But if you gave it the right amount of flow, with properly trimmed policies and reasonable expectations, it became a **miracle box**. A firewall friend. A watchdog sensei. A little box that reminded you that **security isn't about horsepower—it's about awareness, focus, and follow-through**. And that sometimes, the smallest log entries tell the biggest stories.

9. Of course, the IDP-50 wasn't perfect. Its Java-based management interface required patience and a ritual sacrifice to the browser gods. Throughput was modest, and tuning was a must. You didn't throw it in front of 500Mbps fiber connections and expect a miracle. But you also didn't expect a housecat to fight off a bear. You deployed the IDP-50 **where it made sense**—at branch offices, in labs, in tactical deployments, or places where bigger boxes just wouldn't fit. And for those environments? It was **perfect**. Stealthy, skilled, and surprisingly snarky.

10. In the grand hierarchy of Juniper Jitsu, the IDP-50 earned its black belt in subtlety. It was the **packet monk** of the IDP clan—watching, logging, alerting, and occasionally striking with grace. It taught admins the value of tuning. It reminded organizations that detection doesn't have to be massive—it just has to be **meaningful**. It caught threats that firewalls missed. It generated insights that made policies smarter. And it did all of that with fewer resources than your average smart fridge. That's not just impressive—that's **legendary**.

11. For many admins, the IDP-50 was their **first introduction to serious intrusion detection**. It didn't overwhelm. It didn't demand. It just offered clarity. You could follow attack chains, trace reconnaissance attempts, and monitor application misuse with surgical precision. And because it didn't come with overwhelming features or intimidating complexity, it became the ideal learning platform. Small teams, solo admins, and security newcomers all found value in this unassuming box. It didn't teach with flash—it taught with **facts**. It didn't shout—it observed. And what it showed you? You never un-saw.

12. Perhaps its greatest strength was its **lack of pretense**. The IDP-50 never claimed to be a datacenter beast. It didn't pretend to do deep learning or quantum inspection. It did what it said on the tin—**detect intrusion and prevent nonsense**, all in a box the size of a paperback. There was an honesty to it. A humility. And that made it trustworthy. When you checked the logs, you *believed* what it told you. That kind of relationship? It's rare in network security.

13. The end of life for the IDP-50 came quietly, as all good senseis deserve. No fireworks. No farewell tour. Just a deprecation notice, a firmware update, and the gradual migration of policies to SRX-based AppSecure. But even as it left the stage, the IDP-50 left behind **a new standard for compact, effective detection**. Its spirit lived on in branch deployments, lightweight IPS profiles, and the belief that "small" doesn't mean "weak." And those of us who used it? We kept one on a shelf somewhere. Just in case. Just to remember.

14. So let us bow deeply to the **IDP-50**. The silent log-writer. The underdog anomaly detector. The tiny titan that watched the wire while others watched dashboards. It didn't need applause. It didn't need marketing. It just needed **a place to plug in, a few packets to parse, and a mission**. And when it got those? It *delivered*.

15. One of the most charming qualities of the IDP-50 was its **complete lack of ego**. It didn't hog resources, demand flashy dashboards, or require a five-node cluster to feel important. It was perfectly content with its role: **watch the line, protect the edge, and keep the logs clean**. It didn't care that the datacenter had shinier toys or that someone just deployed an AI-powered sandbox with a marketing team larger than most SOCs. The IDP-50 just blinked gently in its corner, flagged that sketchy IRC traffic coming from the intern's laptop, and carried on like the **packet monk it was born to be**. You could ignore it—until you couldn't. And that's when it'd save your bacon with a signature match and a log line so crisp it deserved its own applause.

16. Administrators quickly learned that the IDP-50 wasn't just a "deploy-and-forget" device—it was a **teacher in disguise**. It taught you how to **tune rulesets**, interpret alerts, and understand what "normal" traffic *actually* looked like. And once you knew normal, you started spotting weird without even trying. That moment when you noticed outbound TCP on port 25 and said, "That's not right,"—yeah, thank the IDP-50 for training those instincts. Its raw, unfiltered honesty in detection output gave rise to **pattern recognition superpowers** in any admin who bothered to read more than the first ten log entries. And every false positive? A lesson. Every alert storm? A fire drill. Every accurate match? A little bit of joy.

17. The IDP-50 made **remote security operations possible** for organizations that didn't have SOCs or full-time infosec staff. Its tiny form factor and manageable UI meant you could **ship it out, plug it in, and monitor it centrally**. With NSM or syslog consolidation, you could detect threats at dozens of locations from a single console. And while the IDP-50 didn't have AI, ML, or a voice assistant, it had **consistency**—and in security, consistency beats cleverness nine times out of ten. It offered security that scaled across a business without requiring fire-breathing infrastructure or budget meetings filled with tears. It was **democratized defense**—small-scale intrusion prevention that made even the tiniest offices feel like Fort Knox (with slightly worse coffee).

18. It's hard to overstate how **cost-effective** the IDP-50 was compared to its impact. It didn't need a network redesign, dedicated support team, or even a whole rack. You just needed a flat surface, a working port mirror (or inline path), and someone willing to log in once a week. The value it delivered per dollar, per watt, and per byte inspected was, in many cases, **better than appliances costing ten times more**. Not because it could do more, but because it did exactly what was needed. No fluff. No fanfare. Just **focus and function**.

19. Its **integration into layered security models** was also a hidden gem. You could pair the IDP-50 with an SSG or SRX firewall, letting the big box handle NAT and routing while the tiny box sniffed for foul play. It didn't care who took the credit—it just needed the traffic. In many deployments, the IDP-50 operated like a **canary in the Ethernet coal mine**, flagging abnormal behavior that warranted deeper investigation. And in complex environments with compliance constraints, its presence checked boxes you didn't even know needed checking. Layered security isn't about having *more* boxes—it's about having the *right* ones. And the IDP-50? Was often the right one.

20. Troubleshooting with an IDP-50 was a bit like **interrogating a witness who only spoke in truth bullets**. You didn't get flow diagrams or animated threat maps. You got logs. Beautiful, brutal, timestamped, detail-packed logs. If you read them carefully, they told stories: who tried to go where, when they did it, what they sent, and how badly they failed. With enough familiarity, you could tell the difference between user error, malware behavior, and just plain weirdness with a single glance at a session log. And that kind of visibility was invaluable—especially when **nothing else in the stack noticed a thing**.

21. While bigger boxes were trying to learn the meaning of DPI, the IDP-50 was already living it. Application-layer inspection wasn't a novelty—it was its **entire personality**. It spoke fluent HTTP, understood FTP quirks, dissected SMTP like a forensic pathologist, and stared down malformed DNS requests with a tired sigh. It didn't need a separate "app-aware" module—it already *was* aware. That awareness meant it wasn't easily tricked. Encoding tricks, fragmented payloads, double-escaped strings, ancient exploits trying to look like modern packets—**none of it worked**. If the IDP-50 let it through, it was either legit—or **you wrote your policy wrong**.

22. In cybersecurity war stories, the IDP-50 doesn't get enough love. But it should. It's the device that caught someone port scanning the C-suite subnet from a guest Wi-Fi printer. The one that flagged outbound DNS tunneling during a lunch hour. The one that got installed "temporarily" in a test lab and was still running five years later, faithfully logging every weird outbound POST request from that forgotten dev box named "temp-final2b." It didn't have uptime competitions. It just **won by default**.

23. If you ever walked past a rack, saw an IDP-50 wedged between a switch and a modem, and smiled… congratulations. You're one of us. You know the joy of **efficient security**, of doing more with less, of small tools with big power. You remember updating signatures on a Friday afternoon and catching something nasty by Monday morning. You remember copying log entries into Slack and watching your team gasp. You remember a time when **security wasn't about buzzwords—it was about results**. And the IDP-50 delivered results.

24. As newer platforms took over, and as Juniper transitioned deep inspection into the SRX line, the IDP-50 quietly bowed out. No fireworks. No heroic sunset. Just a firmware archive, a deprecation note, and a lot of **sad but proud IT people**. Some of us kept them around—test labs, proof-of-concept deployments, nostalgia shelves. Not because they were still needed… but because they were **still trusted**. And in security, that's not just rare—it's sacred.

25. So ends the tale of the **IDP-50**—small in size, mighty in mission, and fondly remembered by anyone lucky enough to deploy it. It didn't need a big chassis to make a big difference. It didn't brag. It didn't blink. It just watched. Warned. Acted. And did it all with the calm, competent silence of a true packet path protector. As we move into the **mid-tier muscle of the IDP-200 and 600**, take with you the lesson of the IDP-50: **excellence isn't always loud. Sometimes, it's just plugged in, inspecting quietly, doing the job no one else can.**

Chapter 6: IDP-200/600 – Mid-Tier with a Black Belt

1. If the IDP-50 was the stealthy scout of the Juniper Jitsu order, then the **IDP-200 and IDP-600** were the silent enforcers—mid-sized appliances with just enough hardware muscle to handle real traffic while keeping their zen. Built for **medium-sized enterprises, branch datacenters, and security-conscious campuses**, these devices offered a perfect balance of **performance, flexibility, and deep-packet-dismantling know-how**. They weren't here to make noise—they were here to **catch evil mid-flow, mid-payload, and mid-fib**. Each was powered by the same legendary IDP engine that drove the bigger 800 and 8200 series, just tuned to match their sleeker size. And despite being middleweights in the lineup, they hit like heavyweights when properly configured. These appliances made **serious intrusion detection accessible** to networks that didn't have a full SOC or the budget for an entire rack of blinking boxes. If you needed real visibility without a six-figure invoice, the 200 and 600 were ready to train, detect, and drop malicious sessions like a wireless printer drops connections.

2. From a hardware standpoint, the IDP-200 and IDP-600 delivered **everything you needed —
and nothing you didn't**. They came with **Gigabit Ethernet interfaces**, a healthy amount of
RAM, and enough processing power to handle full-stream reassembly, signature inspection, and
session tracking simultaneously. These weren't "prosumer" boxes pretending to be secure — they
were purpose-built for **network-layer martial arts**. The IDP-200 was ideal for smaller networks
and edge sites, while the 600 served as a step up for larger offices or as the backbone for multi-
segment inspection. Both ran **no-frills form factors** — not flashy, not loud, and definitely not
afraid of a little inline mode action. Fans whirred quietly, power lights blinked stoically, and
ports transmitted packets like well-trained warriors on a mission.

3. Like all good Jitsu masters, the IDP-200/600 didn't just look the part — they came packed with
practical, hardened capabilities. First up: **deep inspection via full protocol decoding**.
Whether it was HTTP, FTP, SMTP, POP3, DNS, or the mystical Application-X-sneaky-variant,
the IDP knew how to decode, disassemble, and evaluate traffic down to its metaphysical intent.
Signatures were matched not just on payload patterns, but **on decoded behaviors**. So that
malformed DNS query trying to cause a buffer overflow? Caught. That base64-encoded reverse
shell hidden in an SMTP payload? Seen, flagged, and (if configured) **terminated with
prejudice**.

4. Just like their smaller sibling, the IDP-200/600 operated in **inline, tap, and transparent
bridge modes**, making them incredibly versatile. Need passive monitoring in a sensitive
environment? Tap mode had your back. Want to deploy them inline at your WAN edge to enforce
policy on the fly? Done. Need stealthy detection without touching IP addressing or breaking
legacy routing? Transparent mode was there, whispering, "I see all." These devices were **as
flexible as your network needed them to be**. Drop them into existing topologies, wrap them
around key VLANs, or sit them quietly in observation mode — they didn't complain. They
adapted. And that's the kind of warrior you want watching your packets.

5. Signature support in the IDP-200/600 was full-strength — **no diet, no decaf, and no
disclaimers**. Every update from Juniper's STRIKE team was fair game: malware families,
botnets, reconnaissance patterns, app misuse, and policy violations. You could enable or disable
categories, fine-tune thresholds, and assign different actions based on context. Want to log
everything from the "Evasion" category, but drop everything from "Critical Exploits"? Easy.
Want to create a custom rule that flags suspicious curl commands sent to internal APIs? Go for it.
These boxes didn't just detect — they allowed you to **shape your detection philosophy**. You
were the sensei now. And they followed your lead.

6. Logging and alerting were the **bread and butter** of these mid-tier IDP machines. You could
forward logs to **NSM**, syslog, or SNMP, or you could just watch the alerts scroll by like a live
security movie (with occasional comedy and horror elements). Each log entry gave you source,
destination, protocol, signature match, action taken, and payload context. These logs were **dense**

but readable—like a very serious novel written by someone who loves packets more than people. Alert storms could be tamed with event suppression and thresholds, and filters made it easy to find the true threats hiding in the background noise. If your SOC needed clarity, the IDP-200/600 were ready to narrate the entire packet saga, one TCP session at a time.

7. Where these devices truly shined was in their ability to **enable confidence in policy enforcement**. You didn't need to hope your firewall blocked something—you could **see** it happen. You could trace it. Verify it. Justify it. When security engineers presented to leadership, they weren't guessing. They were referencing real, timestamped logs that said, "This shellcode was blocked at 14:03. Here's the payload. Here's the source. Here's the packet ID." And that kind of confidence? Priceless. Especially when compliance knocks or incident response goes full DEFCON.

8. Network performance was always a concern, but the IDP-200/600 were **surprisingly efficient** —especially after tuning. Out of the box, you got full inspection with a reasonable default policy. But smart admins learned to trim the rulebase, prioritize critical threats, and leave out categories that didn't apply to their environment. You didn't need VoIP signature inspection in an office with no VoIP. You didn't need Oracle exploits flagged in a company that still thinks PostgreSQL is a social media platform. The trick was to make the **appliance match the mission**, and once you did? These IDP mid-tiers were *buttery smooth*. Packet latency stayed low, throughput stayed high, and the logs stayed relevant.

9. Management was done through **IDP Device Manager (for solo missions)** or **NSM (for the multi-appliance ninja compound)**. NSM let you manage multiple IDPs, build and deploy policy templates, track changes, and view event summaries in ways that didn't make your eyes bleed. Sure, it wasn't always the prettiest interface, but it was **solid, scriptable, and reliable**. You could deploy signature updates across all boxes with a click, clone policy sets, and track attack trends over time. It may have looked like a 2005 Java project (because it was), but it worked. And that made all the difference.

10. If you were really feeling brave, you could take the IDP-200 or 600 and **put it in full auto-block mode**—no logging-only, no hand-holding. Just raw, rule-driven enforcement. When tuned well, this mode was like having a digital bouncer that didn't take bribes and knew Kung Fu. But if you misconfigured it or forgot to whitelist certain behaviors? Well, congratulations—you just blocked your CEO from Salesforce. That's why smart admins always tested policies in **monitor mode first**, reviewed logs, tuned exceptions, and then enabled blocking when they were ready. Because nothing inspires humility like dropping half your VPN traffic with a single misconfigured signature.

11. One underrated superpower of the IDP-200 and 600 was their **policy layering**. You didn't need to apply one monolithic wall of detection logic—you could segment rules by zone, direction, protocol, or even schedule. That meant you could be stricter after hours, lenient for guest Wi-Fi, and downright ruthless for anything crossing from untrust to internal. Time-based policies? Check. Interface-specific tuning? Absolutely. You could treat the marketing subnet like the kindergarten playpen it was, while putting the finance VLAN under an inspection regime that would make Sun Tzu proud. And when something weird happened, you could *pinpoint* exactly which rule allowed it and where your logic slipped. This kind of control was rare. And once you had it, it was hard to go back.

12. Deployment of these mid-tier masters was also **shockingly non-disruptive**. Unlike some appliances that required architectural sacrifices and a ceremonial diagram burning, the IDP-200/600 could be slid into most topologies with minimal fuss. Tap mode let you observe without risk. Inline mode offered surgical enforcement. And transparent mode meant you didn't even have to re-IP your unicorn-like legacy subnets. Many admins got their start with these boxes by simply watching. And after a few weeks of "Whoa, what is that doing on port 53?", they realized **visibility is power**. Soon, enforcement followed. And attackers got nervous.

13. These devices weren't just reactive—they enabled **proactive defense**. With the right tuning, you could create honeypot triggers, detect scanning patterns, and alert on anomalies that most tools dismissed as "business as usual." Did your coffee machine just send a DNS query to Russia? Flagged. Is someone running `nmap` during a lunch break scan-athon? Blocked. Is Karen in HR trying to install LimeWire again? *Logged, quarantined, and probably sent to a Slack channel titled "Why Karen."* With mid-tier IDP appliances, you weren't just playing defense—you were **calling plays**.

14. The IDP-200 and 600 also taught admins a valuable lesson: **packet size doesn't predict impact**. A 60-byte ICMP payload could carry more risk than a 4GB movie download. And these appliances didn't fall for superficial metrics. They inspected every session, analyzed the behavior, and made judgment calls based on **real threat potential**. That's what made them dangerous to attackers. You couldn't sneak in something small and hope it got ignored. The IDP saw you. It *understood* you. And it wasn't impressed.

15. One of the more entertaining features of these boxes was their **alerts and logs**, which—when aggregated—looked like a horror novel written by your own network. Things you thought were fine turned out to be nightmares. Printers phoning home. IoT devices probing adjacent VLANs. Legacy apps using insecure protocols like it was still 1999. And suddenly, your "quiet little network" looked more like a **cybersecurity haunted house**. But that was the point. You can't fix what you can't see. And these boxes **made sure you saw everything**.

16. When it came to compliance, these appliances were **audit darlings**. The detailed logs, structured reports, and built-in policy categorization made it easy to map detections to frameworks like **PCI-DSS, HIPAA, and NIST 800-53**. You could prove data wasn't just protected—it was watched, logged, and judged every step of the way. Need to show that unauthorized application traffic is being blocked? There's a policy for that. Want to prove you detect malware callbacks and exfil attempts? There's a log for that too. These mid-tier boxes didn't just help with security—they helped with **credibility**.

17. Of course, no device is perfect, and the IDP-200/600 had their quirks. If overloaded with traffic or under-tuned, they could cause **session delays or drop legitimate traffic**, especially in inline mode. Management via NSM occasionally felt like **trying to teach Java to a cat**. And false positives could creep in if you weren't diligent about tuning and signature updates. But all of that was manageable with experience. The platform didn't promise magic—it promised **results**. And if you respected its limits, it delivered exactly that.

18. One neat trick in the IDP toolbox was its ability to **log and alert without dropping**, making it an excellent intelligence-gathering tool even in permissive environments. You could deploy it in networks where active blocking was politically tricky or operationally risky, and still gain enormous visibility. In those deployments, the IDP wasn't your enforcer—it was your **spyglass**, showing you where the threats were and how they behaved before you wrote the first drop rule. This helped security teams build consensus, justify budget, and demonstrate risk *with receipts*.

19. It's important to recognize how **ahead of its time** these mid-tier IDPs really were. When they launched, most security appliances were focused on port numbers and handshake patterns. But these boxes? They were decoding sessions, matching behaviors, and enforcing complex logic across stateful flows. They weren't just firewalls with a hobby—they were **true intrusion prevention systems,** long before that became a marketing buzzword. They earned the title. And they wore it proudly.

20. There's a quiet kind of pride that comes from catching something with the IDP-200 or 600. You see an alert in the log, follow it through, confirm the behavior, and **stop the attacker cold**— often before anyone else even knew there was a problem. That's a feeling you don't forget. The box may not have had RGB lights or cloud dashboards, but it gave you something more important: **the truth**. And in a world full of noise, that's everything.

21. Over the years, these devices were deployed in **some of the strangest, most creative network topologies known to man**. Behind load balancers. In front of industrial control systems. Mirrored off test networks. Running next to IoT lighting platforms that nobody wanted to admit still existed. And through all of it, they stayed calm, stayed stable, and **kept collecting the evidence**. If packets moved, these boxes saw them. If sessions started, they judged them. And if something smelled fishy? They raised the alarm.

22. Even today, many IDP-200 and 600 units still live in dusty server rooms, blinking gently as they catalog the sins of a thousand subnets. Officially EOL? Maybe. But **unofficially alive and alert**. These are the appliances that keep working long after vendor support ends, firmware updates stop, and everyone else forgets what port they were plugged into. They're like old samurai—scarred, silent, and **still lethal**. You don't decommission an IDP that still sees packets. You thank it. And you keep it plugged in.

23. Admins who learned on the IDP-200 and 600 became **serious defenders**. They learned how to troubleshoot packet flows, read intrusion logs, and build actionable security policies based on real-world behavior. They stopped being afraid of complexity—and started **harnessing it**. These appliances didn't just protect networks. They trained warriors. They were dojo tools as much as they were security boxes. And anyone who spent time with one walked away stronger.

24. So let us raise a metaphorical sake glass to the **IDP-200 and 600**—the mid-tier masters of mayhem detection. They weren't flashy. They didn't demand attention. But they delivered clarity, capability, and calm in the chaos. They earned their black belts not through power, but through **balance**. They stood between the small and the mighty, the unknown and the unthinkable—and did their jobs without complaint. The firewall might have said "deny," but the IDP whispered, "Here's why."

25. And with that, we bow to the mid-tier masters and look ahead to Chapter 7—**IDP-800: The Unsung Wallflower Warrior**. Bigger, bolder, and even better at catching what others missed… if only someone had remembered it was plugged in.

Chapter 7: IDP-800 – The Unsung Wallflower Warrior

1. Sitting squarely between mid-tier elegance and data center drama, the **IDP-800** was Juniper's quietly capable champion—a box with muscle, grace, and a habit of being left out of marketing slides. It wasn't the smallest, nor the biggest, but it delivered **exactly what was needed** in most real-world networks: dependable, flexible intrusion detection with just the right amount of attitude. It ran the full IDP engine, supported custom signatures, and handled modern threats like a polite but terrifying librarian— *"Excuse me, that payload is inappropriate. Session terminated."* The IDP-800 never bragged. Never asked for attention. And yet, it saw everything. For IT teams that didn't have time to babysit their IDS but still wanted to sleep at night, this was **the unsung hero** in their racks.

2. From a hardware perspective, the IDP-800 was **no slouch**. With multi-core processing, decent RAM, and full gigabit throughput support, it had everything it needed to chew through traffic like a disciplined cyber-carnivore. It featured copper and SFP interfaces, standard 1U form factor, and just enough fan noise to reassure you it was still working without becoming the office white noise machine. The front panel was unassuming. The rear? Full of potential. It didn't demand attention, but if someone tried to move it without authorization, it would **log the event,**

flag the user, and probably judge your cabling. It was a perfect fit for medium-to-large organizations looking for inline or mirrored traffic inspection without busting the budget—or the power bill.

3. Like its IDP siblings, the IDP-800 supported **inline, tap, and transparent bridge modes**. Inline gave you full prevention powers—dropping, blocking, and scrubbing traffic with precision. Tap mode offered visibility without risk, great for deploying it behind a span port and just watching the nonsense unfold. Transparent mode? That was your stealth play—no IP addressing, no topology changes, just **ninja-mode packet scrutiny**. Flexibility was one of its defining traits. Whether you were protecting a VLAN, monitoring inter-VRF traffic, or guarding a link between two hostile business units, the IDP-800 fit in and got to work.

4. Where the IDP-800 really shined was in **multi-segment deployments**. With a few interfaces configured and some thoughtful policy writing, you could monitor multiple points in your network from one box—each with its own inspection profile. You could tune rulesets for guest Wi-Fi, internal departments, and cloud uplinks *on the same appliance*. That made the IDP-800 an excellent **consolidation play**. Why deploy three sensors when you could just configure zones, set up some virtual routers, and let the 800 do its thing? It didn't mind the extra work. It thrived on it.

5. Signature support? Full tilt. The IDP-800 received every update Juniper's STRIKE team produced. Zero-days? Yep. Botnet behaviors? Got 'em. Exploit kits, app misuse, policy violations, and weird packet structures that made TCP cry? The 800 was on it. And just like its brothers, it let you customize signatures, enable or disable rule categories, and create **fine-grained response logic** for each detection scenario. Want to log some threats, drop others, and just politely close a session if a user gets frisky with their torrent client? All doable. And the 800 kept it all running without blinking.

6. But despite its power, the IDP-800 often found itself in the strangest role of all: **overlooked**. It didn't get the fanfare of the IDP-8200. It wasn't small enough to be cute like the IDP-50. It sat in the middle, doing all the work, **silently catching reconnaissance attempts while everyone else blamed the printer**. In some environments, it ran for years without anyone logging into the UI. And yet, when you pulled the logs? Dozens of blocked shellcode payloads, hundreds of malware detections, and at least one terrifying outbound DNS exfil attempt from a "sandbox" that clearly had opinions. The IDP-800 was the network equivalent of *the quiet kid in class who aces every test*.

7. The UI experience was typical of its generation: **functional but not exactly thrilling**. Whether you used IDP Device Manager or NSM, you could configure policies, deploy signatures, and track alerts. NSM gave you centralized control across multiple IDPs, while Device Manager was perfect for single-appliance deployments. Neither interface would win beauty contests, but they *worked*. And once you learned where everything lived—*policy tree* *here, event filters there, signature library buried six clicks deep but rich with content—*you were good to go. In fact, the only time the UI became dramatic was during large policy pushes, which occasionally froze with the intensity of a philosophical dilemma.

8. Logs from the IDP-800 were, as expected, **clean, readable, and rich with context**. Each detection gave you source IP, destination IP, protocol, severity, signature name, action taken, and even helpful "why we flagged this" summaries. You could sort by attack category, export to CSV, or integrate with your SIEM for real-time detection feeds. And if you weren't using NSM? The logs were perfectly digestible via syslog, letting your Splunk dashboard sing like a caffeinated bard with packet paranoia. Alerts were detailed, timestamped, and deeply satisfying—especially when the appliance caught something your EDR didn't.

9. In terms of performance, the IDP-800 was **deceptively strong**. Tuned properly, it could handle **hundreds of Mbps** of full inspection traffic with negligible latency. Overload it with signatures? Sure, you'd notice some packet stutter. But keep the rules tight, filter for relevance, and monitor flow counts, and the 800 just purred. Session handling was robust, protocol decoding was reliable, and memory usage rarely spiked unless someone decided to scan the entire subnet during a vulnerability assessment they "forgot" to announce. And when things got heavy? The 800's logs didn't panic—they simply noted, flagged, and moved on. Like a true black-belt.

10. The IDP-800 also played an essential role in **SOC enablement**. For teams just standing up threat detection for the first time, it offered **actionable alerts without analysis paralysis**. Its accuracy meant fewer false positives. Its policy tuning meant junior analysts could learn what *real* threats looked like. And because it was predictable, it trained engineers to **trust the tool**. That alone made it worth its 1U footprint. The IDP-800 wasn't a learning curve—it was a **lesson plan**.

11. If there was one word to describe the IDP-800's detection style, it was **balanced**. It didn't jump at shadows, and it didn't snooze through SQL injections either. Its **signature engine was mature**, its behavior analysis thoughtful, and its event responses calm, collected, and never hysterical. You didn't get alert spam from misbehaving printers unless they were genuinely threatening your subnet's sovereignty. And when something **truly suspicious** happened—say, an outbound reverse shell wrapped in base64 from an internal dev server—it didn't panic. It flagged. It logged. It optionally slapped the session into next week. It was a **sober second opinion** in a world of firewalls that either blocked nothing or *everything*.

12. Perhaps what made the IDP-800 such a quiet hero was its **consistency across environments**. Drop it into a healthcare network? It watched HL7 traffic like a hawk. Throw it into a university? It quickly learned to separate prank scans from real attacks. Put it at the WAN edge of a retailer? It quietly clocked hundreds of policy violations per day—mostly from poorly patched POS systems. In every case, the 800 adapted. It didn't complain. It just **reassessed risk and stayed sharp**. And because it never overreacted or missed the obvious, it earned the trust of admins who'd long since stopped trusting their firewall logs.

13. Tuning policies on the 800 was an **exercise in elegant control**. Want to block P2P across the whole network but allow certain VPNs through? Easy. Need to flag, but not block, potential lateral movement between VLANs? Done. The policy tree let you stack detection rules logically, with overrides, category weights, and custom exceptions. And the custom signature engine? Just *chef's kiss*. Regex wizards, rejoice. With a bit of effort, you could make the 800 detect **anything that moved in a suspicious rhythm**, from data exfiltration to rogue API usage to Gary running Telnet *again*. (We told him.)

14. Over time, some security teams began to see the IDP-800 as more than a device — it was a **mentor**. It taught you what your network really did when you weren't looking. It exposed the weird, the risky, and the downright ridiculous. It pushed junior analysts into learning TCP/IP the hard way. It taught incident responders the art of reconstructing a breach timeline from logs alone. And when a big detection hit and the whole team rallied? The IDP-800 was already logging the next anomaly. No glory. No blinking red sirens. Just **dedication and discipline**.

15. Another unsung strength was its role in **cross-platform correlation**. The IDP-800's logs, when piped into a SIEM or analytics engine, added **meaningful context** to what other devices saw. Your firewall might block an outbound connection. Your endpoint might flag a suspicious process. But the 800? It told you what actually went down the wire, *which payload triggered what signature*, and *whether the response was blocked, logged, or ignored*. It was the **missing link** in a lot of otherwise-disconnected security architectures. And for that, it often became the most valuable tool in the SOC — without ever needing a firmware update.

16. Its use in **regulated industries** couldn't be overstated either. Whether you were dealing with **SOX, HIPAA, PCI-DSS, or NERC**, the IDP-800 helped tick boxes not with checkmarks, but with **confidence**. It enforced detection on encrypted tunnels, application misuse, and insider threats. It helped detect unauthorized protocol use, like TFTP over strange ports, or SMB traffic attempting cross-zone jumps. And when the auditor said, "Prove to me you're monitoring internal threat vectors," the IDP-800 calmly dropped a PDF on the table with **timestamps, packet data, and an entire taxonomy of mischief**. Auditors blinked. Admins smiled. Boxes got ticked.

17. Its high-availability options were modest but functional. You could configure failover behavior, redundant paths, and syslog redundancy to avoid data loss during a reboot. And while it wasn't built for clustered performance like the IDP-8200EX, you could pair it with another for resilience. That meant **less risk during upgrades** and **more uptime during chaos**. No one wants their IDS to reboot mid-breach, and the IDP-800's stable platform ensured it rarely had to. But when it did, it did so with **grace, logs intact, and no tantrums**.

18. Custom application recognition also made the 800 a favorite for **tailored security policies**. You could define what "normal" looked like, not just in terms of ports and protocols, but

application behavior, session duration, and packet cadence. Want to flag long-lived DNS queries? Track excessive HTTP POSTs with small payloads? Flag users who try 20 SSH logins in under 30 seconds? All possible. The 800 let you speak your own detection dialect, and it listened attentively. It turned even the most obscure network habits into **trackable insights**.

19. Over time, the IDP-800 also became a **stepping stone into larger security strategies**. Teams that outgrew it didn't discard it—they **graduated**. They moved to the 8200 or transitioned to SRX with AppSecure, but they carried the **lessons** with them. Policy hygiene. Signature tuning. Session decoding. Behavior baselining. These weren't just features—they were skills taught by a humble box that looked like it belonged in a quiet closet, not the security war room. And yet, it shaped defenders like few tools could.

20. As newer platforms emerged, the IDP-800 began its quiet fade into EOL status. Support was phased out, firmware updates stopped, and new deployments gave way to SRX systems with baked-in AppID engines. But the IDP-800 never complained. It didn't rage. It didn't throw logs at the wall. It just… kept working. And for many, that meant **years of bonus protection**—unsupported, yes, but still sharp, still accurate, and still doing the job.

21. Even today, if you ask old-school Juniper admins which box they miss most, many will say, "The 800." Not because it was flashy or fancy—but because it was **reliable**. It didn't crash. It didn't overpromise. It did exactly what it was told, and then some. It was the security appliance equivalent of the friend who helps you move, doesn't eat your pizza, and brings their own dolly. **Trustworthy. Solid. Always shows up.**

22. You can still find IDP-800s in the wild—quietly watching traffic in forgotten branch offices, unplugged but kept "just in case," or running in test labs to teach the next generation of packet whisperers. They may not get firmware updates anymore, but their **value hasn't diminished**. A tuned, functioning IDP-800 is still more useful than a dozen modern "AI-driven" appliances that haven't been configured properly. And unlike the modern stuff, it **doesn't make you agree to 19 pages of licensing just to inspect port 443**.

23. So what did we learn from the IDP-800? That security doesn't need to be loud. That insight comes from context, not clutter. That real-time protection is about **precision, not panic**. And that sometimes, the most important device in your rack is the one that hasn't crashed, hasn't complained, and has been **silently catching shellcode since 2009**.

24. The IDP-800 was a **silent wallflower** only in form. In function, it was a beast. It scanned quietly, reported precisely, and enforced firmly. It didn't ask for headlines. It didn't get an awards show. But it got the job done—and made a lot of defenders look brilliant in the process. You may not notice it at first. But once you see what it's capable of? You'll **never want to be without it**.

25. Thus ends the tale of the IDP-800: *The Unsung Wallflower Warrior*. Modest in appearance, mighty in performance, and eternally underappreciated. It was the box that didn't just catch packets—it caught careers, trained defenders, and reminded us all that the most powerful warrior is the one who doesn't

Chapter 8: SRX Begins – The Unified Field Theory of Firewalls

1. The arrival of the **SRX Series** was less a product launch and more a **philosophical shift**. Juniper didn't just release new boxes—they announced a new way of thinking: what if routing, firewalling, VPNs, intrusion prevention, and next-gen visibility all existed under one OS? One command set? One terrifyingly deep hierarchy of curly braces? Welcome to the **Unified Field Theory of Firewalls**—also known as **JunOS**. The SRX line merged the best of Juniper's legacy (think NetScreen policy logic and IDP threat detection) with the **robust routing power of the MX and the configurational panache of the EX series**. The result? A beast of a security platform that could do nearly anything—**as long as you remembered to "commit."**

2. The SRX wasn't a single device. It was a **pantheon**. From the branch-friendly **SRX100 and SRX300** series to the data center juggernauts like the **SRX5400, SRX5600, and SRX5800**, the product line scaled like a security samurai dojo—from fresh recruits to masters of mayhem. Each SRX ran JunOS, meaning configuration was modular, feature-rich, and sometimes deeply meditative. Want to build a zone-based policy firewall with VPN, NAT, UTM, and IDP on the same box? No problem. Want to also run BGP, multicast routing, and tie it into a chassis cluster? Sure. Just remember: **if you don't commit, it didn't happen**.

3. At the heart of the SRX was **JunOS**—an operating system equal parts powerful and occasionally mystifying. Unlike ScreenOS, which offered fast, flat config lines like a shotgun blast of logic, JunOS introduced **a hierarchical structure**, XML-like syntax, and **a level of indentation discipline that would make Python blush**. Policies were still zone-based, but now lived in "security" stanzas. Interfaces were tied to security zones through logical constructs. NAT had its own policy hierarchy. And the CLI? Polite, contextual, and ready to autocomplete your deepest desires—as long as you knew where you were in the config tree. It was a new world. But once you mastered it? **You could wield firewall power like a true packet mage.**

4. One of the most dramatic evolutions SRX brought was its **modularity**. Especially in the high-end series, you didn't just get ports—you got **slots**, each housing **services processing cards (SPCs)** and **network interface cards (NPCs)**. This allowed you to scale processing power separately from I/O, tailor hardware for your specific needs, and swap components faster than a LARP enthusiast gearing up for firewall combat. Even the smaller branch SRX models came with modular options: expansion ports, SFPs, and software licenses that unlocked features like **AppSecure**, **UTM**, and **advanced VPN capabilities**. No more buying a new box just to get five more VPN tunnels. Now you could **upgrade with intention**.

5. In the SRX realm, **AppSecure** was the crown jewel of modern inspection — Juniper's answer to the app-aware future. No longer satisfied with port/protocol combos, AppSecure identified applications based on behavior, heuristics, and deep packet sleuthing. Want to block Facebook but allow Messenger? Done. Want to throttle Dropbox uploads but allow Google Drive? Possible (and oddly satisfying). The SRX didn't just look at the IP header — it **read the soul of the stream**. AppSecure came with AppFW, AppQoS, and AppTrack — all designed to classify, log, shape, or smash applications into submission. With the right tuning, it made the SRX feel less like a firewall and more like a **network therapist**: observing behaviors and gently suggesting improvements... or blocking them outright.

6. But AppSecure was just the start. The SRX also integrated **IDP**, meaning you could inspect packets deeply, surgically, and on schedule. Like its IDP-box predecessors, this engine used signatures, protocol decoders, and anomaly detection. The difference? Now it lived inside your firewall. No need for a second box, another power outlet, or a separate management platform. It brought all the **Layer 7 insight of the IDP-800** and rolled it into a unified security policy. And yes — you could still customize signatures, prioritize threats, and *politely close sessions of misbehaving traffic*.

7. Management on SRX was as flexible as its config. You could use the **CLI**, of course — the natural habitat for many network senseis. Or you could pivot to **J-Web**, a lightweight GUI that let you configure, monitor, and commit without touching the terminal. For larger environments, Juniper offered **Junos Space Security Director**, a centralized platform that could deploy policy to dozens or hundreds of SRX devices, track logs, view threat maps, and occasionally freeze at the worst possible time. And for those truly in tune with the JunOS spirit, you could automate deployments with **Python, Ansible, or Juniper's own PyEZ library**. The SRX wasn't just a box. It was a **lifestyle**.

8. Speaking of logs — the SRX wrote logs like a network poet. Security logs. System logs. Flow logs. Debugs. Alerts. You name it. Want to know if a session dropped, why it dropped, who dropped it, and how long it sulked before timing out? It's there. The logs weren't just verbose — they were **truthful**, often revealing problems faster than packet captures. Want to track every SSH connection over the last 72 hours? AppTrack's got you. Want to know how many users are abusing DNS for tunneling? AppFW + logs = enlightenment. Just don't forget to rotate your logs. Because verbosity... is a blessing and a burden.

9. The **zone-based policy structure** remained the spiritual backbone of SRX, a clear continuation of the NetScreen and SSG heritage. You created security zones. You attached interfaces. You wrote policies "from trust to untrust," or from DMZ to VPN, or from marketing to everywhere (deny). Each policy could match source, destination, application, user, time, or even custom tags. It was intuitive once you got the hang of it—and **brutally effective** once you mastered it. SRX didn't make assumptions. If traffic wasn't explicitly permitted, it didn't go through. Like a bouncer who checks the guest list twice, then stares at you until you back away.

10. One thing you quickly learned on SRX was that **order matters**. Not just in policies, but in NAT, firewall filters, route resolution, and even how you paste configurations. A misordered NAT rule could break a VPN faster than you could say "rollback." A misplaced security policy could open your datacenter to the public faster than an intern learning wildcard masks. But the SRX gave you tools: **"commit confirmed"**, **"show pending,"** and **"rollback N"** to save you from yourself. It knew that even masters sometimes typo. It didn't shame you—it gave you the means to undo, reflect, and try again.

11. Another defining feature of the SRX family was **scalability without ceremony**. Start with a humble SRX100 at the branch? Sure. Need to upgrade to an SRX1500 or an SRX4600 for enterprise edge traffic? Go ahead. The syntax stayed the same. The philosophy remained constant. Whether you were defending ten endpoints or ten thousand, the SRX spoke one dialect: **JunOS**. That meant learning once and leveling up for life. New gear didn't mean new chaos—it just meant more horsepower. And when you finally moved into the chassis-based SRX5800? The CLI still greeted you like an old friend… right before it inspected 120 Gbps of traffic like a sentient brick wall.

12. High availability was baked into the SRX's DNA. You didn't need to juggle extra licenses or buy a mystery box from a third-party vendor. With **chassis clustering**, you could pair SRXs together into active/active or active/passive failover mode—syncing sessions, NAT tables, routing info, and even firewall state. Failovers were smooth. Seamless. Sometimes you didn't even know it happened until you saw the log: *Node 1 took over from Node 0. Everyone remained calm.* SRX HA wasn't just for show—it was real redundancy, tested in the field, and trusted in places where uptime was sacred.

13. VPNs on SRX? *Chef's kiss.* Full support for **IPsec site-to-site**, **dynamic VPN**, and **SSL VPN (in some models)** made it a versatile VPN hub. You could use IKEv1 or IKEv2, preshared keys or certificates, and set up route-based or policy-based tunnels depending on your mood and masochism. With a few well-placed stanzas, you could tunnel half the planet's traffic through a single SRX and still have CPU to spare. And if something broke? Logs. Beautiful, detailed, phase-1/phase-2-loving logs. No more guessing which side failed. SRX told you. Calmly. Respectfully. With just a hint of judgment.

14. NAT on the SRX was a full-blown **choose-your-own-adventure experience**. You had **source NAT**, **destination NAT**, **static NAT**, **proxy-ARP**, and **port-overloading tricks** that made old-school NetScreen admins weep with joy. But you also had the freedom—and burden— of deciding where NAT happened in the chain of operations. Pre-routing? Post-policy? It was all there… you just had to plan your logic. SRX gave you power and responsibility, which is to say:

if you accidentally NAT'd your DMZ webserver to your coffee machine, that was on *you*. But when NAT was done right? It was **surgical, seamless, and stupidly satisfying**.

15. One of the biggest cultural shifts the SRX introduced was its embrace of **"next-gen" mindset**—long before it was plastered on every vendor's datasheet. By combining firewalling, routing, application awareness, and user identity, the SRX became more than just a box in the rack. It became the **nerve center of the network perimeter**. And as enterprises evolved, so did SRX. Cloud connectors, REST APIs, and automation hooks allowed it to plug into modern pipelines without looking like a relic. It wasn't just protecting the network. It was **part of it**. That's the kind of integration that turned casual users into **fanatical believers**.

16. Performance across the SRX family was nothing short of **heroic**—especially on higher-end models with dedicated SPCs. You weren't just pushing packets; you were **marching them through a full parade of services**: AppSecure, IPS, NAT, routing, logging, threat detection, QoS… all while hitting line rate. And the CPU? Barely sweating. Load-balancing across cores, distributing flow sessions intelligently, and offloading crypto to dedicated hardware modules meant that SRX didn't just keep up with traffic—it **orchestrated it**. You could throw 10G links, BGP tables, and app filtering at it all day. It wouldn't blink. But it might judge your ACL naming conventions.

17. And then there was **logging**. If logs were gold, SRX was Fort Knox. Everything—from session initiation to teardown, NAT translation, app detection, VPN handshake stages, and signature hits—was logged in glorious detail. You could forward it all to syslog, stream it to Security Director, or pipe it into your favorite SIEM. Want to troubleshoot why DNS broke at 3:47 a.m.? The SRX had **twelve logs for that**. Need to prove to an auditor that the VPN dropped a session due to inactivity timeout and not human error? Done. This wasn't logging. This was **a detailed historical record of every digital decision the box ever made**.

18. Juniper also made sure SRX wasn't just a security device—it was **an automation-friendly, dev-savvy powerhouse**. With **RESTful APIs**, **NETCONF support**, and **Juniper PyEZ**, the SRX became a programmable endpoint in your network automation strategy. You could write Python scripts to manage config snippets, push policy changes via GitOps, or dynamically open firewall ports based on security events. This wasn't just convenient—it was transformational. You no longer had to SSH into every box and copy/paste like it was 2005. The SRX spoke JSON, XML, and YAML. It was ready to be **versioned, templated, and unleashed**.

19. The SRX also introduced **user-based firewalling**, giving you control over not just devices, but identities. Integration with Active Directory allowed policies based on users and groups— "Allow Finance to SAP, block everyone else." Combine that with AppSecure and QoS, and suddenly you could **treat users like the traffic citizens they were or weren't**. If Gary in Marketing abused Spotify during peak hours, his traffic could be shaped with a vengeance. If the

CEO needed access to an obscure cloud app, the SRX could accommodate. This wasn't just security—it was **network karma enforcement**.

20. As SRX adoption grew, the box earned its place not just in racks, but in **network culture**. Engineers began to reference "commits" in everyday conversation. Automation workflows were designed around its policy logic. Slack channels filled with `show security flow session` screenshots. It stopped being "a Juniper firewall" and started being **the infrastructure cornerstone**, the device you built around. It was where your VLANs converged, where your tunnels terminated, where your policies lived. And it did it all without raising its voice.

21. Of course, SRX had its quirks. Overly nested configuration trees. The occasional "Why won't this route redistribute?" mystery. And yes, that moment where you accidentally deleted a policy stanza and only realized after a live `commit confirmed 1`. But those moments didn't erode trust. They built wisdom. The SRX wasn't a toy—it was a **tool for disciplined practitioners**. You didn't brute force it. You **understood it**. And when you did, it returned the favor by securing your world.

22. For teams transitioning from legacy firewalls, SRX was **a rite of passage**. You struggled with the hierarchy. You wrestled with commit errors. You spent way too long renaming an interface. But then it clicked. And when it did? You wielded security policy with a level of **grace and precision** you didn't know was possible. The box didn't just level up your network. It **leveled up your team**.

23. Even as the cybersecurity landscape changed—with cloud-native firewalls, containerized workloads, and zero-trust architectures—SRX remained **relevant, ready, and resolute**. It plugged into AWS and Azure. It supported virtual editions. It adapted to orchestrators. It wasn't a legacy box—it was a **legacy of evolution**. One built on policy logic, user trust, and the idea that great security isn't about guessing… it's about knowing, inspecting, and deciding.

24. The SRX family proved that **unification didn't mean compromise**. You could have routing and firewalling. App inspection and performance. Modularity and stability. It wasn't about "or" —it was about **"and."** It was the first Juniper platform that felt like a thesis: all the experience, lessons, and quirks of the past boiled down into one versatile, cohesive, utterly overpowered piece of network gear. And once you got good with it? There was no going back.

25. Thus concludes the story of **SRX Begins**—a chapter not just in hardware, but in mindset. The SRX didn't just defend networks—it shaped them. Trained teams. Taught patience. And delivered clarity in a world full of fuzz. It was the **unified field theory of firewalls**, and it turned

Chapter 9: SRX100 – Ninja Training Wheels

1. In the vast dojo of SRX appliances, the **SRX100** stood out not for its power, but for its **potential**. It was the firewall equivalent of a wooden practice sword—compact, affordable, and completely capable of teaching you how not to chop your own leg off. Designed for **small offices, remote branches, and first-time JunOS users**, the SRX100 was Juniper's official "getting started" box, and boy did it deliver. It gave you zones, policies, VPN, NAT, and even light UTM features in a form factor that could survive being shoved into a server closet next to dusty switches and forgotten Sonicwalls. It wasn't flashy. It wasn't fast. But it was **fearless**. And it was the perfect place for a networking student to begin their SRX journey.

2. The SRX100 came in a few flavors—B, H, and H-M—but the essence was the same: **8 ports, 1U of rackless charm, and a CLI that led you gently into the JunOS jungle**. It wasn't built to handle gigabits of encrypted traffic, but it could hold its own against most office-sized threats and bandwidth demands. It ran full JunOS, so anything you learned on the 100 would apply when you graduated to SRX240s, 550s, or even the almighty 5800. This was Juniper's ultimate teaching tool: a device so friendly and accessible it practically handed you a katana and whispered, *"You're ready."*

3. One of the first things new admins noticed about the SRX100 was how **quietly confident** it was. No loud fans. No blinking LEDs that screamed for attention. Just a soft hum and the occasional blinking status light that let you know it was there, doing firewall things. The CLI was your main interface, and while it required some initial learning, it quickly became **a language of power**. Every `set security policy` command felt like casting a spell. Every `show configuration | display set` revealed the inner harmony of your network. And that first successful commit? *Pure enlightenment.*

4. The SRX100 wasn't content to just be a firewall—it came equipped with **routing superpowers** that made it a viable core router for small networks. Full support for **static routes, OSPF, RIP, and even BGP** meant you could build dynamic environments even in branch deployments. Want to dual-home a site? Done. Want to peer with the mothership over MPLS and still route guest Wi-Fi to a crummy DSL link? The SRX100 didn't flinch. It was more than a perimeter defender. It was **a traffic whisperer in a compact box**.

5. NAT was handled with grace and clarity, and—unlike in ScreenOS—it actually made sense after a few tries. You got **source NAT, destination NAT, and static NAT**, plus the flexibility to choose between interface-based, pool-based, and policy-based approaches. Sure, you'd probably

NAT the wrong thing the first few times (welcome to the club), but with a few `show security nat source` commands and some packet captures, the truth always emerged. And once you understood the **flow-based nature of JunOS**, NAT became less of a mystery and more of a **packet art form**.

6. VPN on the SRX100 was where many admins earned their **first bruises — and first victories**. It supported **route-based and policy-based IPsec**, complete with IKE Phase 1/2 tuning, lifetimes, dead peer detection, and more acronyms than a government contract. Getting that first tunnel up took effort. Keeping it up required finesse. But when it worked? *Magic*. Encrypted sessions sailed through, logs confirmed success, and users never knew just how many hours of CLI meditation went into their access to HQ files. This was **real-world ninja training**, and the SRX100 was your sparring partner.

7. Of course, the SRX100 had limits. Push too many UTM features, and its CPU got anxious. Try to route gigabits of traffic with AppSecure enabled, and you'd start seeing log messages that hinted, politely but firmly, that you should slow your roll. But within its limits? The SRX100 was **a reliable, patient, nearly indestructible companion**. It didn't lie about its capabilities. It didn't promise unicorn throughput. It simply said, *"Configure me well, and I will protect you."*

8. The device even supported **basic Unified Threat Management (UTM)** services like antivirus, web filtering, and antispam — though you'd be wise to use these sparingly. They worked, but the box wasn't designed to inspect every packet like a full-on datacenter appliance. This was a **lightweight guardian,** not a heavy-handed brute. And when tuned properly — say, web filtering for guest networks or lightweight AV on outbound traffic — it worked *just fine*. Just don't turn on every feature at once unless you enjoy watching CPU graphs become abstract art.

9. Logging and alerting on the SRX100 were refreshingly detailed, even in such a small package. Security logs captured policy matches, session state, NAT events, and VPN lifecycles. You could forward logs to syslog servers, watch them live in the CLI, or even configure SNMP traps if you were feeling bold. The clarity of logs taught you how the box **thought about traffic** — and that insight made troubleshooting not just easier, but **enlightening**. Log watchers quickly became traffic monks, parsing timestamps like digital tea leaves.

10. One of the SRX100's most defining qualities was how **forgiving it was to new users**. Make a mistake in the config? Roll it back. Forget to attach an interface to a zone? It'll remind you. Delete your entire NAT table by accident? Okay, maybe that one's on you — but the CLI won't let you commit unless your syntax is flawless. JunOS trained you with guardrails, not shackles. The SRX100 became not just a firewall, but a **learning environment**, a CLI dojo, and a judgment-free zone (except for config errors, of course).

11. One of the most elegant parts of the SRX100 was its embrace of **zones**, a concept inherited from its NetScreen ancestors but reimagined in the world of JunOS. You didn't just plug in a port and call it a day—you assigned it a **role**. Trust, untrust, DMZ, guest, corporate—each became a logical security domain. Policies were written between zones, and **traffic obeyed those policies with military precision**. This wasn't "allow all, hope for the best" firewalling. This was **intent-based design**, and it made even the smallest branch feel like it had a security team hiding behind every port.

12. As organizations grew, the SRX100 gracefully stepped into **branch-office backbone duty**. You could connect it to MPLS circuits, Internet uplinks, VoIP subnets, and VPN tunnels simultaneously. It handled static routes, participated in dynamic routing protocols, and even supported multicast if you needed to stream traffic like it was 1999. The best part? It never broke a sweat. Well, unless you tried to run full IDS, UTM, and a crypto-heavy VPN over a DSL line during a Zoom call. But even then? It didn't reboot. It didn't complain. It simply whispered, "Maybe don't."

13. For security teams just building out their playbooks, the SRX100 became an **experiment station**. Want to test split tunneling with dynamic VPN? It's in there. Curious about application-layer controls with AppSecure? Supported—if lightly. Need to learn how to write firewall filters, attach CoS classifiers, or even use RADIUS authentication for user-based policies? Yep. The SRX100 didn't just allow you to experiment—it **encouraged** it. It was the firewall equivalent of a padded room with CLI access. And for admins, that kind of safe space was invaluable.

14. It also taught one of the most important lessons in networking: **the power of clarity**. With JunOS, everything was explicit. Nothing happened by accident. You configured it. You committed it. You reviewed the result. And when something broke, the logs were honest. There was no hand-holding, no "guess what went wrong" interfaces. The SRX100 helped junior engineers become **deliberate**, **precise**, and **thoughtful**—skills that scale far beyond firewalls.

15. High availability on the SRX100 was limited, but still possible. You could configure **redundant links, VRRP**, and basic failover policies. For a device of its size, that was plenty. No chassis clustering here—just **solid reliability and graceful degradation**. Power it through a UPS, give it a static route to a backup WAN, and you had a tiny resilience platform that could shrug off most branch-level outages. It wouldn't win awards for uptime architecture. But it didn't have to. It just worked.

16. When paired with centralized management via **Junos Space Security Director**, the SRX100 could become part of a larger security fabric. You could push policy, monitor logs, and roll out changes from a single pane of glass—turning your SRX100 fleet into a **distributed force of packet samurai**. Did it require some licensing and prep? Yes. Did it scale well for businesses with dozens of branches? Also yes. And that's when the SRX100 became more than a firewall—it became an **agent of consistency**.

17. Over time, the SRX100 built a **cult following**. Not because it was flashy. Not because it was powerful. But because it taught people **how to firewall properly**. It was like your first real guitar —not the loudest or prettiest, but the one that taught you chords, calluses, and confidence. Admins grew up on the SRX100. It turned interns into engineers and engineers into security architects. For many, it was **the first box they truly understood**—and that understanding stuck.

18. It also held up well over the years. Firmware updates kept it relevant far longer than expected. Newer SRX models emerged, boasting more power and shinier features, but the SRX100 still blinked faithfully from under desks, in network closets, and on lab benches. In an industry addicted to refresh cycles and shiny new things, the SRX100 was a testament to **endurance through usefulness**. You didn't replace it because it broke. You replaced it because you outgrew it—and even then, you usually kept it around *just in case*.

19. One of the most charming quirks of the SRX100 was its tendency to **teach through failure**. Misconfigure a policy? It didn't warn you—it simply enforced it. Break your NAT? Enjoy learning flow sessions in real-time. Commit a half-finished change during a live tunnel migration? Say hello to rollback. These weren't problems. They were lessons. And because the device was so stable, so transparent, and so readable, you could recover, reconfigure, and retry without fear. The SRX100 didn't judge. It just watched. And helped.

20. For many small businesses, the SRX100 was their **entire security perimeter**—firewall, VPN concentrator, routing hub, and sometimes even DHCP and DNS helper. That's a lot of hats for one box, but the 100 wore them with quiet competence. It didn't mind doing everything. It just expected you to know what you were doing. It wasn't about power—it was about **balance**. And in most deployments, it found that balance beautifully.

21. Even the J-Web GUI on the SRX100—long the subject of grumbles from CLI purists— offered **a friendly learning ramp**. You could browse interfaces, monitor sessions, adjust NAT, and even build basic policies without touching the terminal. Was it clunky? Yes. Was it helpful? Also yes. Especially for teams new to JunOS or transitioning from GUI-only environments. And once you grew confident? The CLI was always waiting. Like a black belt, ready to show you the way.

22. There's something special about the SRX100's legacy. It didn't just defend packets—it **created practitioners**. It wasn't just a firewall—it was a **rite of passage**. If you knew how to configure an SRX100 from scratch, write a working VPN, and troubleshoot policy flow by reading the logs? You weren't just competent. You were initiated. And whether you moved on to SRX300s, 1500s, or full-blown 5800 chassis monsters, you brought those lessons with you.

23. Today, the SRX100 has largely stepped back from the front lines. Officially EOL. Replaced in most deployments. But unofficially? It lives on in labs, in test benches, in teaching racks, and in the fond memories of admins who knew what it meant to start small, configure carefully, and defend honorably. You'll still find them—blinking away under desks, routing guest Wi-Fi, or guarding IoT VLANs from printer-based chaos. Because **you don't just throw away your first katana**.

24. So let's honor the SRX100—the ninja training wheels of the Juniper Jitsu world. It asked for nothing but care. It gave you everything: skills, confidence, insight, and a deep appreciation for the power of structured configuration. It didn't do everything. It didn't have to. What it did was **make you better**. And that's more than most gear can say.

25. Thus ends the story of the **SRX100**: small in form, rich in wisdom, and the firewall equivalent of a sensei who let you fail just enough to grow. As we move forward into larger branch deployments, we meet its ambitious sibling in **Chapter 10 – SRX240: Gateway Guardian of Growing Networks**. The wheels are off. The VPNs are longer. And the training montage continues.

Chapter 10: SRX240 – The Low-End Linebacker

1. If the SRX100 was the nimble scout of Juniper Jitsu, the **SRX240** was its beefier, burlier big brother—a device that looked at branch traffic and said, "Yeah, I can take that hit." This was the firewall that showed up with cleats on. A solid upgrade from the 100 series, the SRX240 brought **more ports, more throughput, and more headroom for packet punishment**. It was still small-office friendly, but it was built for sites that saw more than just cat memes and the occasional VPN check-in. Retail locations, school districts, law offices, and regional headquarters? This was their go-to. It didn't just scale up. It **grew up.**

2. The SRX240 came in several variants over the years: the base model, the "H" (high-memory), and the occasionally misunderstood "B" model, which was basically the SRX240 after a weekend of strength training. With **16 Ethernet ports**, two mini-PIM slots, and optional power redundancy, this thing had **serious I/O street cred**. You could plug in access switches, DMZ servers, VoIP gear, and backup WAN links without blinking. It was the first SRX that felt less like a friendly appliance and more like a **network bouncer** that moonlighted as a policy enforcer.

3. The jump from SRX100 to SRX240 wasn't just physical—it was philosophical. With more power came **more responsibility**: UTM was no longer theoretical, AppSecure actually worked, and IDP wasn't just a checkbox in a feature matrix. You could actually run deep inspection without choking the CPU. Sure, you still needed to be careful (don't throw full UTM, IDP, and 15 IPSec tunnels on it at once), but with thoughtful config, it hummed along like a **Zen linebacker**, calm and crushing.

4. One of the most practical benefits of the SRX240 was its ability to **segment networks with ease**. With all those ports and the flexibility of zones and VLANs, you could turn it into a miniature datacenter core: guest Wi-Fi on its own VLAN, VoIP on another, POS terminals isolated like the fragile things they are, and a DMZ that's actually demilitarized. This wasn't just a firewall; it was a **network architecture class in a box.**

5. Routing was where the SRX240 started showing its Juniper DNA. It handled **OSPF, BGP, RIP, and static routing** like a champ. And with support for virtual routers, you could run multiple routing instances side-by-side—great for multi-tenant setups or complex WAN environments. Branch office with dual WAN and MPLS? No problem. School district with a central fiber uplink and per-site segmentation? Easy. This was **big router energy** in a firewall shell.

6. VPN capabilities were rock solid. Whether you needed **site-to-site tunnels, dynamic VPN for road warriors, or even GRE tunneling**, the SRX240 had your back. It supported IKEv1 and IKEv2, full Phase 1 and 2 customization, and enough logging to troubleshoot misaligned PSKs in your sleep. Once you built a few VPNs on the 240, you developed **a sixth sense for dead peer detection and lifetime mismatch errors.** It wasn't just a VPN device—it was a **crypto dojo.**

7. AppSecure on the SRX240 actually had **room to breathe.** You could enable AppTrack, AppFW, and even AppQoS without the entire box collapsing into a puddle of dropped packets. Application visibility brought clarity to chaos: "Hey, 60% of our bandwidth is YouTube, 20% is Dropbox, and 10% is Steve in accounting playing online poker." AppSecure turned the SRX240 from a wall into a **window.** You didn't just block threats—you understood them.

8. IDP was no longer a marketing feature; it became a **real option**. You could apply inspection profiles to interfaces, set thresholds, enable signature categories, and even write custom attack detection rules. Signature updates via Juniper's STRIKE feed gave it a steady diet of fresh intelligence. And when tuned correctly, IDP on the 240 could **see the punch coming and block it mid-swing**. You wouldn't run a full-blown SOC on this thing, but you *could* make attackers cry.

9. Management options on the SRX240 expanded as well. CLI remained king, but J-Web was more functional than on earlier models. For larger environments, **Junos Space Security Director** allowed centralized policy management, and syslog exports worked beautifully with modern SIEMs. Logs were verbose, insightful, and sometimes poetic: "*Session denied due to policy. Source: Gary. Destination: Everywhere. Reason: Obvious.*" It was a joy to read—unless you were Gary.

10. With its modular PIM slots, the SRX240 allowed **hardware customization** too. Want fiber uplinks? Add an SFP PIM. Need 4G backup? Cellular mini-PIM, baby. Juniper gave you just enough modularity to solve real problems without turning it into a Frankenfirewall. This was practical expandability, not a money grab. And every time you slid in a module and it just worked, you felt like a **network MacGyver**.

11. As the network grew, so did the expectations on the SRX240. And it usually delivered. It could handle **dozens of active VPN tunnels, thousands of sessions**, and moderate amounts of UTM and AppSecure without falling over. Sure, there were limits. Push it too far and you got the dreaded memory threshold alerts. But respect the box, and it would **guard your packets like a linebacker guards the end zone**.

12. SRX240 also brought **real-world survivability** to the table. Field deployments included dusty warehouses, sweltering telecom closets, and that one branch office that inexplicably ran its gear next to the employee microwave. The 240 didn't care. It just booted up, kept state, and **blocked traffic like a caffeinated doorman**.

13. From a logging and analytics perspective, the SRX240 could make your SIEM feel like a clairvoyant. Session logging, policy hits, dropped traffic, and application usage flowed freely into Splunk, LogRhythm, Graylog, or whatever poor open-source solution you were forcing into production. Need insight on weird DNS activity? It's in there. Want to trace a suspicious outbound connection? Already logged. **This was visibility, not guesswork.**

14. Performance tuning became part of the SRX240 admin's journey. You learned when to shape traffic, when to disable ALG features, and how to configure flow-based versus packet-based forwarding depending on your loadout. You didn't just configure the 240 — you **trained with it**. Each tweak was a kata. Each optimization, a form of firewalling tai chi.

15. And of course, it wasn't perfect. Boot times were... contemplative. Interface naming conventions occasionally contradicted logic and physics. And firmware upgrades sometimes felt like **a trust fall in a dark alley**. But once patched and humming, the SRX240 rarely needed hand-holding. It was a firewall, not a diva.

16. In multi-site environments, SRX240s formed **the backbone of distributed defense**. Easily deployed, centrally managed, and highly consistent, they enabled security teams to roll out policies with surgical precision across an entire WAN. You could build templates, push updates, and standardize logging — **the foundation of any disciplined digital martial art**.

17. You also couldn't overlook the **bang for buck**. For its price point, the SRX240 delivered serious horsepower and flexibility. You got a true zone-based firewall with routing chops, VPN flexibility, application control, and solid IDP — all wrapped up in a rugged chassis that said, "Yeah, I can handle your regional office. Try me." It wasn't the cheapest. But it **earned every dollar**.

18. Engineers who trained on the SRX240 carried those skills forward. Understanding zones, policies, NAT precedence, and traffic flow on this box meant you could configure bigger SRXs with ease. You weren't just learning a model. You were learning a philosophy. And every `commit confirmed` was another step toward **packet enlightenment**.

19. Over time, as newer SRX models like the 300 and 1500 series came out, the 240 stepped back—but not without fanfare. Even in retirement, it remained beloved in test labs, dev networks, and budget-strapped remote offices. Many lived on, blinking away in racks long after support ended. Because you don't retire **a linebacker** just because they get a little gray around the config.

20. So here's to the **SRX240**: a firewall that taught, protected, and carried more than its share. It was overbuilt, under-hyped, and fully capable. It didn't ask for praise. It didn't need applause. It simply **held the line**.

21. When a site went down, and the only thing left working was the SRX240? You knew it had your back. When policy changes made the cloud angry, but traffic still flowed? The 240 stood firm. It was the kind of firewall you could depend on—and the kind you missed when it was gone.

22. In a world full of flashy dashboards, subscription bloat, and clickbait UIs, the SRX240 was **a firewall for the serious practitioner**. No fluff. No drama. Just clean, purposeful defense. It made you better. And it expected you to act accordingly.

23. Its place in Juniper Jitsu is one of **grit and reliability**. It didn't flip through app signatures like a dating app. It studied them. Understood them. Blocked what mattered. Logged what didn't. And moved on.

24. Let future engineers speak of chassis clusters and AppID microservices. Let them marvel at SD-WAN overlays and cloud-native firewalls. But let them also remember the SRX240, and the admins who learned to wield it with skill, restraint, and the occasional `run clear log messages` when things got messy.

25. Next up: **Chapter 11 – SRX300: Leaner, Meaner, and Made for Modern Branches.** The new era is upon us. But never forget the linebacker that cleared the path.

Chapter 11: SRX650 – Midrange with Muscle

1. If the SRX240 was the linebacker, the **SRX650** was the linebacker's older cousin who lifts freight trains for fun and reviews routing tables for breakfast. Squarely in the **midrange powerhouse category**, the SRX650 brought serious processing muscle, modularity, and scalability to branch and campus networks that didn't want to compromise. It wasn't quite a data center beast, but it could definitely bench press a small one. Ideal for large branches, regional hubs, or small enterprises with big dreams, the 650 was **Juniper's not-so-subtle message**: "Yeah, we do heavy lifting, too."

2. At first glance, the SRX650 looked like someone crossed a firewall with a small-business server: **2U of rugged chassis**, modular slots, a no-nonsense faceplate, and vents that whispered, *"I process packets faster than you can scream 'zero-day'."* It supported multiple **Services and**

Network Processing Cards (SPCs and NPCs), had **hot-swappable fans and power**, and enough ports to host a LAN party for an entire Fortune 500 team. This wasn't plug-and-play. This was **rack-and-attack.**

3. Power was the name of the game. The SRX650 delivered up to **7 Gbps of firewall throughput**, **2 Gbps of IPS**, and thousands of concurrent VPN tunnels without flinching. It could route, inspect, log, filter, and encrypt all in the same breath. And thanks to dedicated hardware acceleration for crypto and flow processing, it didn't just keep up—it **ran laps around older platforms**. You didn't babysit a 650. You unleashed it.

4. The modular architecture made it feel like **a grown-up SRX**, one that could evolve with your network. Need more fiber ports? Swap in an SFP interface module. Want to isolate VLANs by physical interface? Add another line card. Demand power redundancy? Slide in that second PSU. Unlike fixed-platform boxes, the SRX650 **grew with your ambition**, offering just enough flexibility to feel enterprise-grade without requiring a PhD to install.

5. Like all SRXs, the 650 ran **JunOS**, and that meant all the glorious config consistency you'd come to love (or fear). CLI was king, rollback saved lives, and commits were sacred. Everything from **zone-based policies to AppSecure to IDP** lived within the same logical structure. And when you "show interface terse" on a box with 40 active ports and custom VLAN tagging, it felt like **peering into organized packet chaos**.

6. The 650's sweet spot was its ability to be **many things to many admins**. A branch firewall. A core router. A VPN concentrator. An IDP engine. It could sit quietly at the edge, act as a perimeter guardian, or even **take the throne as the campus security gateway**. Its session capacity and concurrent flow handling meant it could absorb traffic spikes, security events, and that one user streaming 4K cat videos during a patch deployment.

7. VPN support was top-tier. You had your **standard IPsec**, your **dynamic VPNs**, your **route-based tunnels**, and every IKE tweak imaginable. It handled large-scale VPN deployments like a champ and gave you **debug output so detailed it could double as bedtime reading for security engineers**. Configuring VPNs on the SRX650 turned junior admins into crypto philosophers: *"Is this peer group actually our true identity, or just a phase 1 illusion?"*

8. AppSecure truly flourished on this platform. With ample memory and processing, the SRX650 could run **AppTrack, AppFW, and AppQoS** across multiple interfaces simultaneously. Want to throttle Netflix? Done. Want to block Tor? Sure. Need to understand what SaaS apps are chewing up your pipe? AppSecure didn't just tell you. It **drew you a map and highlighted Steve's laptop.**

9. IDP on the 650 was no joke. It came with **full STRIKE signature support**, customizable rule sets, and the power to enforce inline without compromising performance. You could tune detection profiles, assign threat priorities, and enable **real-time packet protection** without turning your throughput into soup. When deployed correctly, it became **your own private NOC bouncer** – clipboard, earpiece, and all.

10. The SRX650 didn't just do logs. It performed **event symphonies**. Session logs, NAT translations, policy matches, VPN events, IDP hits, application detections—they flowed in real-time to your SIEM, syslog, or on-box buffer like a jazz solo in TCP. Whether you were troubleshooting a failed VPN handshake or tracking down unauthorized DNS tunneling, the logs were clear, coherent, and brutally honest. This was **truth at wire speed**.

11. For deployments that demanded uptime, the SRX650 offered **redundancy without ridiculousness**. Hot-swappable fans and power supplies, support for VRRP, and full chassis cluster mode meant your firewall could survive hardware failure, WAN drops, and intern-induced outages. It wasn't bulletproof. But it **wasn't going down without a very loud fight.**

12. From a design standpoint, the 650 was the **perfect midpoint** between the old-school IDP appliances and the mega SRX beasts. It carried the detection torch forward while embracing unified architecture. It had enough interfaces to impress your network architect and just enough aesthetic to look intimidating in a rack. You didn't hug this box. You **saluted it**.

13. Configuration best practices mattered here. If you didn't know your way around flow processing, ALG settings, or firewall filters, the SRX650 would happily educate you—usually via dropped sessions and a growing log file titled "Oops.log." But once you dialed it in, the 650 rewarded you with **unshakable reliability and ironclad control.**

14. It also introduced many admins to **advanced high availability concepts**, like RTO/RP path monitoring, preemptive failover, and session syncing between cluster nodes. These weren't just buttons you clicked—they were disciplines you practiced. And every failover test that *didn't* cause user complaints felt like **a small enlightenment**.

15. Perhaps most importantly, the SRX650 prepared engineers for the big leagues. If you mastered it, **SRX1500s, 3400s, and 5000s** suddenly looked far less intimidating. It was a training ground and a proving ground. It gave you real-world experience with real-time consequences. And it did so with a smirk and a blinking power light.

16. The learning curve wasn't gentle. It didn't come with guardrails. But once you got past the initial configuration gauntlet, you had **an all-in-one security appliance** that could protect, shape, and inspect traffic better than most boxes twice its price.

17. Budget-wise, the SRX650 punched well above its weight. Mid-sized businesses got enterprise-level features. Regional networks got datacenter vibes. And engineers got hands-on experience with true platform modularity. The only thing it lacked was a marketing campaign worthy of its chops.

18. For many organizations, the SRX650 was **the first firewall they trusted enough to forget about**. Not because they didn't monitor it—but because it rarely needed fixing. It became part of the furniture, humming away, inspecting packets, logging anomalies, and letting everything else take the credit. That's how **quiet legends** are made.

19. Eventually, the SRX650 passed the torch to newer models with sleeker lines and faster processors. But those who deployed one never forgot. Like an old martial arts master, the 650 aged out of combat but remained in the dojo—watching, teaching, and occasionally showing a newer model how it's really done.

20. So raise a config file to the **SRX650**: the midrange marvel, the mod-friendly beast, the box that taught engineers how to work smarter and firewall harder. It didn't blink. It didn't boast. It just **protected**.

21. When the alarms went off and packets flew wild, the SRX650 stood tall, checked its logs, and **let the policy do the talking**. That's not hype. That's legacy.

22. In the next chapter, we climb higher up the performance ladder with the **SRX1400**. It's faster, louder, and more fun than a packet storm at a pen test party. But never forget the 650—the middleweight champ who showed up early, stayed late, and **never dropped a packet without a reason.**

Chapter 12: SRX1400 – The Unsung Tank

1. The **SRX1400** was the firewall equivalent of a tank parked quietly at the edge of the network —not flashy, not fast, but incredibly difficult to move, and even harder to kill. Nestled between the mid-tier SRX650 and the god-tier 5K series, the SRX1400 was often overlooked. It wasn't the fastest. It wasn't the sleekest. But it was **relentlessly capable**. For government sites, critical infrastructure, and enterprise backbones that needed something serious but not excessive, the 1400 was perfect. Think of it as the **unbreakable generalist** of the SRX lineage—ready for anything, and built to last.

2. Visually, the SRX1400 looked like a **steel-clad bookshelf with vengeance in its vents**. A 3U chassis that screamed, "I dare you to misconfigure me," it featured **modular I/O**, **hot-swappable power**, and **front-to-back airflow** designed to survive the most grizzled of data centers. It was rack-mount royalty—no-nonsense, all function. With dedicated NPC (Network Processing Cards) and SPC (Services Processing Cards), this box wasn't just powerful—it was **divinely symmetrical in its modularity**. Want to scale up? Slide in another card. Want more fiber? Swap modules. The 1400 let you **build your destiny.**

3. In terms of performance, the SRX1400 didn't disappoint. With a **firewall throughput of up to 30 Gbps** and **up to 10 Gbps of IPsec VPN**, this thing could shoulder regional traffic loads without so much as a packet hiccup. It handled **millions of concurrent sessions** and **tens of thousands of new sessions per second**. While it didn't compete with the SRX5800 in raw horsepower, it **didn't need to**. It lived in a sweet spot—more muscle than the 650, less overkill than the 5K series, and way more composure under pressure than many of its contemporaries.

4. The SRX1400 wasn't just strong—it was **strategic**. With **high-end crypto acceleration**, support for **chassis clustering**, and full **AppSecure** and **IDP capabilities**, it could morph from edge protector to data center guardian in a single config commit. It scaled for WAN aggregation, branch termination, or inter-data center security. And thanks to its **flexible control plane**, you could carve it into virtual systems, managing multiple security contexts from a single iron beast. This was **Swiss Army security**, forged in titanium.

5. Like its siblings, the SRX1400 ran **JunOS**, which meant full CLI command structure, rollback, and hierarchical configuration so deep it made emacs look shallow. The learning curve remained steep but rewarding. Once you mastered `show chassis cluster interfaces` and `set security policies from-zone this to-zone that` on a box with six NPCs and an angry SIEM waiting downstream, you weren't just an admin. You were a **firewall philosopher-warrior.**

6. Modular design was key. You could mix-and-match **I/O cards**, swap out failed power supplies mid-flight, and even run **SPC upgrades** without fully dismantling the entire platform. The SRX1400 wasn't afraid of change. It **embraced lifecycle extension** like a monk embraces silence. Want to shift from copper to fiber? Do it. Need more IDP horsepower? Add another SPC. Every upgrade was a **ceremony of improvement**, not a forklift upgrade.

7. Logging on the 1400 was as rich and dramatic as a Shakespearean soliloquy. Every session had a tale. Every packet, a story. With proper syslog redirection and Security Director integration, the SRX1400 became a **narrator of the network's soul**. You didn't just see alerts. You **read the evolution of threats**, traced user behavior, and reconstructed data flows like a forensic packet archaeologist.

8. AppSecure wasn't a footnote here. It was a **full-blown revelation**. The SRX1400 had the headroom to run AppTrack, AppFW, and AppQoS without gasping for CPU. Want to prioritize VoIP? It could do that. Need to block YouTube on guest Wi-Fi? With pleasure. Want to alert when someone opens Tor inside your finance subnet? *Already logged it, friend*. This was **application awareness with backbone**.

9. IDP was equally potent. The SRX1400 could ingest signature updates, parse anomalies, and execute mitigation policies **without losing composure or flow state**. Attack detection became less of a game of cat-and-mouse and more of an **automated martial art**, with rulesets so refined they could differentiate between a malformed packet and a clumsy user running Wireshark on the wrong VLAN.

10. Its ability to integrate with **Security Director**, **syslog**, **SNMP traps**, and **external orchestration platforms** made the SRX1400 extremely automation-friendly. Whether you managed it with scripts, templates, or command-line wizardry, it adapted to your workflow. In fact, it often ran better **with orchestration than without**. Like a tank with a GPS and a battle strategy, it knew how to follow orders—and win the war.

11. Redundancy on the SRX1400 was **top-shelf enterprise**. With **chassis clustering**, you could run dual nodes, synchronize sessions, and **failover in milliseconds**. Even when one node failed, the other would pick up where it left off, like a well-rehearsed stunt double. This wasn't just uptime. It was **survivability.**

12. While it didn't have the marketing sparkle of newer SRX models, the 1400 had something rarer: **deep trust from experienced engineers**. It worked. It scaled. It obeyed. And it kept doing so long after its newer siblings started showing signs of subscription fatigue and feature bloat. The 1400 didn't believe in SaaS gimmicks. It believed in **packet discipline**.

13. Despite being discontinued, many SRX1400s still live on in **test labs, outposts, and deeply paranoid environments**. Because when you need a firewall that just works—no drama, no nagging subscriptions, no blinking alerts asking you to "go cloud"--you call the 1400. It doesn't care about trends. It cares about **secure traffic flow**.

14. If you were lucky enough to cut your teeth on the 1400, you didn't just learn firewalling. You learned **resilience, modularity, and meticulous policy writing**. The 1400 was unforgiving if misconfigured, but endlessly dependable when respected. It made good admins better and taught great admins to slow down, breathe, and get their zones right the first time.

15. There were quirks, of course. Boot times were glacial. Config commits on large policy sets could feel like watching tectonic shifts. But when the 1400 finally said "commit complete," it meant it. You could trust it. And in the world of security appliances, **that's sacred**.

16. Engineers often described it as a firewall that "doesn't need your approval." It didn't care what the rest of the infrastructure was doing. It had its job, and it did it with **stoic perfection**. If traffic matched policy, it passed. If it didn't, it vanished like a dishonorable warrior in the mist. No apologies. Just enforcement.

17. When attackers hit, the SRX1400 didn't raise alarms in panic. It raised **one perfect alert, backed by logs, matched to signatures**, and already enacting the policy response. Where other firewalls blinked and buffered, the 1400 just **acted**.

18. In many ways, it felt like Juniper built the SRX1400 for engineers first, auditors second, and marketing never. It wasn't flashy. But it ran for years. It protected assets. It **defended the undefendable**. And it did it all without asking for anything but proper airflow and a clean config.

19. Teams who deployed the 1400 slept better. Not because the threats were fewer, but because the defense was **utterly dependable**. Even in an era of zero-days and ransomware blitzes, the SRX1400 sat in its rack, checking policies, inspecting packets, and **quietly winning.**

20. So here's to the **SRX1400**: the unsung tank, the guardian of mid-enterprise complexity, the firewall that came in peace but was fully ready for war. It didn't blink. It didn't blog. It just **defended**.

21. Next up: **Chapter 13 – SRX1500: Next-Gen Punch in a Compact Form**. We're stepping back into sleek chassis, faster flows, and the new era of integrated security appliances. But never forget the tank that kept the perimeter locked while others were still loading firmware.

Chapter 13: SRX3400 – Twin-Blade Fury

1. If the SRX1400 was a tank, the **SRX3400** was a **dual-bladed attack helicopter**: faster, meaner, and capable of delivering a flurry of security strikes before most firewalls even finished loading their bootloader. With its modular, scalable architecture and unmistakable chassis presence, the SRX3400 made a bold statement: "*I am not here to blink. I am here to block.*" Designed for **large enterprise cores and medium-sized data centers**, it brought together raw performance, surgical control, and multi-layered defense—in stereo.

2. What made the SRX3400 stand out immediately was its **twin-slot architecture**. The name "3400" wasn't just marketing flair—it literally referred to the **dual services blades** it could wield like katanas in the dark. With **up to 30 Gbps of firewall throughput, 10 Gbps of IPsec**, and **8 NPC/SPC slots**, this box didn't just sit in your rack—it **owned it**. It wasn't just designed for throughput—it was built for **parallelized packet domination**.

3. The hardware itself was poetry in motion. Dual power supplies, hot-swappable fans, modular I/O cards, and a control board that quietly judged your cable management. Its 5U form factor screamed "serious business," while its internal airflow and thermal management made it the **server room's best-behaved beast**. You could run this thing in a frozen bunker or a blazing boiler room, and it would still process flows like a seasoned warrior meditating through chaos.

4. At the heart of the SRX3400's prowess was its **distributed processing engine**. Each **SPC (Services Processing Card)** handled inspection duties like IDP, UTM, and AppSecure. Meanwhile, **NPCs (Network Processing Cards)** took care of interfaces, NAT, and flow management. The separation of duties wasn't just a design choice—it was **a security philosophy**. Just like any great martial arts team, everyone had a role, and no one overstepped.

5. With support for **chassis clustering**, the SRX3400 could partner up with another unit to create an **active/active HA pair**. Sessions synced. Heartbeats monitored. Failover? Practically instantaneous. When one node dropped, the other took over so smoothly that your users only noticed because their Netflix stream didn't stutter. (Yes, that's a threat vector now.) This wasn't just high availability. This was **high vigilance**.

6. As always, JunOS kept things consistent and powerful. All your favorite zone-based security structures, AppSecure controls, and IDP profiles were still here, just with **more threads and more teeth**. Writing policies on the SRX3400 was a bit like preparing a tournament bracket: precise, strategic, and fully capable of delivering **payload-purging punishment** to the losing team. Every config felt like setting a trap—and every log confirmed the catch.

7. AppSecure on the 3400 was **fully weaponized**. With enough CPU to handle real-time application identification across multiple interfaces and zones, it could run **AppTrack, AppFW**, and **AppQoS** at scale. Want to block BitTorrent on VLAN 30 while prioritizing Salesforce on VLAN 40? Done. Want to inspect traffic from marketing without affecting finance? Easy. Want to alert when a wild Discord client appears? *Already done, sensei.*

8. IDP? Oh yes. The SRX3400 didn't just support intrusion detection and prevention—it devoured it. Signature updates came in like sacred scrolls from STRIKE, and the SPCs interpreted them with **clinical elegance**. You could apply IDP policies per zone, per interface, or globally. Customize thresholds. Tailor attack categories. Block specific evasion techniques. This wasn't spray-and-pray IDS. This was **a sniping operation wrapped in XML.**

9. The box's **VPN capabilities** were everything you'd expect from Juniper at this tier. Full support for **IPsec, IKEv1/v2**, dynamic VPNs, route-based, policy-based—you name it. The 3400 could terminate **thousands of concurrent tunnels**, making it the perfect VPN aggregation point for distributed organizations. And because logging was so detailed, you could spot renegade endpoints, diagnose key mismatches, or even catch that one intern who accidentally misconfigured their Phase 1 to expire every six minutes.

10. Speaking of logs, the SRX3400 was a **confessional booth for packets**. It logged everything. Session starts. NAT decisions. Policy matches. Threat detections. Application identifications. If it passed through or near the 3400, it was **documented and timestamped**. The logs didn't just tell you what happened. They told you why it happened, what triggered it, and how to prevent it from ever happening again. This was more than monitoring. This was **narrative security**.

11. For automation aficionados, the SRX3400 spoke your language. **NETCONF, REST API, Junos PyEZ**, and all the scripting integration points were there. You could write a Python script to deploy a multi-zone firewall policy, verify interface health, or perform forensic queries against flow sessions. This was **automation with teeth**, and it turned skilled engineers into **cyber-ninjas with config katanas**.

12. And yes, there were quirks. Like all complex platforms, the SRX3400 had its moods. Committing a massive config with nested IDP, AppSecure, and NAT policies could sometimes feel like **summoning a demon with the wrong incantation**. But 99% of the time? It was smooth. And when it wasn't, the logs were honest about your sins.

13. Performance tuning on the SRX3400 was both a science and an art. Know when to allocate SPC cores. Understand session distribution across NPCs. Optimize AppSecure profiles for your actual traffic. With great power came great tunability. But when done right? The 3400 became a **security symphony**, with every module playing in concert.

14. Perhaps the most powerful aspect of the SRX3400 was its longevity. Despite being part of the "older" SRX lineage, it continued to serve in thousands of environments long after newer models showed up with touchscreens and attitude. Why? Because it **still worked. Flawlessly**. And because it could be upgraded, modified, and tuned like a vintage samurai blade.

15. For the engineers who lived with it, the SRX3400 earned **a special place in the dojo**. It was dependable, strong, flexible, and fair. It didn't hold your hand, but it didn't backstab you either. It just delivered. And that kind of consistency in cybersecurity is **rarer than a well-commented NAT policy**.

16. Sure, new platforms came with better UIs, more cloud hooks, and prettier dashboards. But when the breach report hit your inbox, you didn't reach for pretty. You reached for **precise**. And the SRX3400 was nothing if not precise.

17. Field stories abound of 3400s running for **five years without a single reboot**, even as they weathered power surges, software upgrades, and the occasional misplugged fiber from an overconfident junior admin. These weren't just firewalls. They were **digital fortresses**.

18. And so we salute the SRX3400: **the Twin-Blade Fury**, the high-performance monster that brought symmetry to network security and balance to deep inspection. It didn't crave the spotlight. It just took up the sword.

19. Next up: **Chapter 14 – SRX3600: When Fury Gets Fancy**. Because when you double down on SPCs, NPCs, and flow-based excellence, you don't get noise. You get **graceful devastation**.

Chapter 14: SRX3600 – Datacenter-Friendly Fisticuffs

1. If the SRX3400 was twin-blade fury, then the **SRX3600** was that same fury upgraded with **more steel, more slots, and a wider stance**. It was like Juniper took the SRX3400, bought it a power-lifting gym membership, and gave it a bigger rack. Positioned squarely between core and cloud, the SRX3600 was designed to **smash high-throughput bottlenecks**, wrangle service provider traffic, and inspect enough sessions to make even the most daring attacker think twice.

2. The hardware profile made that immediately obvious. The 3600 brought a **7U chassis**, more **SPC/NPC expansion slots**, and **higher throughput ceilings** to the game. With **up to 60 Gbps firewall throughput** and **15 Gbps of IPsec VPN**, this box wasn't kidding around. Fiber-heavy I/O configurations, airflow for days, and power redundancy that could rival a UPS farm made the 3600 feel **at home in a datacenter**, but still comfortable enough in high-end enterprise environments.

3. Modularity remained a core strength. You could stack **NPCs** for interface-heavy workloads and **SPCs** to boost processing muscle. Load balancing across processing cards made scaling feel like assembling a **Lego set with laser turrets**. Whether you were terminating 100+ VPNs, monitoring campus-wide application traffic, or serving as the core security node for a distributed enterprise, the SRX3600 adjusted accordingly. It didn't complain. It **executed.**

4. The control plane was as precise as ever. With a dedicated **Routing Engine**, it separated data from control in a way that ensured **stability during storms**. Whether under DDoS, link failover, or policy chaos, the routing engine just kept handling BGP updates while SPCs carried on with packet inspection like meditative martial artists ignoring background noise.

5. Configuration via **JunOS** was still very much a CLI affair—deep, consistent, and just hierarchical enough to make you question your indentation discipline. But the benefits were clear: **rollbacks, scripting, commit checks, and zone-based segmentation** were all first-class citizens. You didn't babysit this box. You **communed** with it.

6. The SRX3600 was a **session behemoth**, capable of handling **millions of concurrent sessions** and **tens of thousands of new sessions per second**. Flow-based forwarding was optimized with NPCs, while security features like NAT, ALG, and application-layer inspection hummed in the background like an orchestra of digital watchdogs.

7. Speaking of inspection, **AppSecure** on the SRX3600 reached a new level of maturity. It could identify applications **across multi-gigabit flows**, shape traffic with **AppQoS**, enforce policy with **AppFW**, and log everything with **AppTrack**. Want to see how much Office365 traffic is coming from your finance VLAN? It's in there. Want to de-prioritize Spotify during backups? Welcome to the **discipline dojo**.

8. IDP was no longer just an add-on—it was a core competency. With ample SPC resources, you could run full inspection across multiple zones, apply signature categories with surgical precision, and even enable **anomaly detection** for stealthy, behavior-based attacks. IDP on the 3600 felt less like pattern matching and more like **network judo**.

9. As for VPN, the SRX3600 was a **crypto terminator**. With hardware acceleration for IPsec, it could run **high-scale tunnel hubs** without bottlenecks. Whether you were connecting remote branches, third-party partners, or international disaster recovery sites, the SRX3600 made secure comms **look easy**.

10. Chassis clustering turned this into a **two-headed dragon**. Active/active HA, session sync, full failover, and fabric link redundancy made sure that even during power loss or hardware failure, the box didn't just survive—it **kept fighting**. Engineers would joke: *"The SRX3600 won't die unless you actively make it."* And even then, it might reboot and ask, "Round two?"

11. Policy writing was **an exercise in elegance**. With zone-based structures, match conditions, application awareness, and user-based identity policies, you could create firewalls so intelligent they knew which user was trying to access Dropbox from which VLAN and **why that was a bad idea**. It wasn't just about blocking. It was about **precision-guided control.**

12. Logging was like reading a philosophical novel written by packets. You got session lifecycle details, NAT translations, policy decisions, threat matches, and application signatures, all timestamped and ready to be digested by SIEMs or log collectors. The box didn't just report. It **reconstructed events**.

13. And let's not forget the **performance tuning fun**. With customizable inspection profiles, traffic shaping, interface-level policies, and resource-aware flow tuning, you could tune this box like a street racer prepping for a showdown. Once dialed in? The SRX3600 was **network performance poetry.**

14. Unlike lighter boxes, the 3600 thrived in **complex environments**. MPLS cores? Check. Multi-zone multi-VLAN DMZs? Done. Segmentation for regulatory compliance? Easy. You could deploy it in everything from public sector racks to banking data centers and it would blend in like **a packet-processing ninja in a suit**.

15. Automation was smooth. REST, NETCONF, PyEZ, and template-driven config structures meant it played well with modern orchestration stacks. Want to deploy HA clusters from Ansible? Go for it. Need to automate config backups and compliance checks? Already done. This box didn't just sit there — it **contributed to the workflow**.

16. Reliability was baked into its bones. The SRX3600 ran for **years without intervention**, even in environments with high temperature, high traffic, and low patience. It wasn't a diva. It was **a disciple**.

17. There were a few quirks. Module recognition occasionally required a firmware nudge. IDP updates sometimes acted like moody teenagers. And SNMP traps needed a good stern talking-to. But nothing that couldn't be resolved by an admin who'd read the manuals and sacrificed a config stanza or two to the firewall gods.

18. Engineers who worked on the SRX3600 came away with **battlefield discipline**. They learned how to build HA pairs, optimize flow logic, and debug NAT issues in the middle of config push chaos. You didn't just deploy the 3600. You **graduated from it**.

19. It didn't chase trends. No one bought it for the GUI. They bought it because it was **modular, configurable, and willing to meet you halfway if you brought your A-game**. This wasn't a consumer firewall. It was **a professional tool for packet samurai**.

20. If the SRX650 was midrange with muscle, the 3600 was **upper-midrange with menace**. It straddled the line between enterprise deployment and datacenter bouncer. It didn't look for trouble. It **waited for it.**

21. For many companies, it was the first time they felt **in total control of traffic**. Not just blocking ports and scanning flows, but **understanding usage, enforcing behavior, and architecting trust**. That kind of clarity only comes from a system that isn't afraid of complexity. It **relished it**.

22. Eventually, the SRX3600 bowed out, replaced by newer, shinier, cloudier models. But the legacy endured. Boxes remained online in test beds, DR sites, and hardened facilities. Because while others aged, the 3600 just kept blinking and **inspecting like it was 2011.**

23. Admins who knew the 3600 could walk into any firewall conversation and speak with authority. Not because they had memorized commands, but because they understood intent. The box had taught them that. It was **more mentor than machine**.

24. So here's to the SRX3600: the datacenter bruiser with the heart of a philosopher. It didn't talk much. But when it did? You read the logs. And you **listened.**

25. Next up: **Chapter 15 – SRX5800: The Summit of Stateful Security**. Hope you brought climbing gear. We're heading to the top.

Chapter 15: SRX5400 – Core Network Katana

1. Enter the **SRX5400**, the firewall that doesn't just guard the gates—it *sharpens the blade and dares the enemy to try*. This was Juniper's first swing into the high-end SRX5K series, and it hit like a katana through spaghetti code. The SRX5400 was compact in the family, but powerful enough to secure **major enterprise cores, regional data centers, and critical cloud ingress points**. It was where throughput met elegance—and where security policies came to meditate with steel.

2. At 5U tall, the SRX5400 was **smaller than its 5800 sibling**, but don't let that fool you. It supported **four midplane slots**, allowing a mix of **SPCs (Services Processing Cards)** and **NPCs (Network Processing Cards)** that scaled up throughput and inspection muscle without unnecessary fluff. With up to **480 Gbps of firewall throughput** (when fully loaded), this box could **slice through traffic bottlenecks like a hot blade through bad ideas.**

3. Aesthetically, it was all business. The faceplate looked like it belonged in a weapons locker. LEDs? Subtle but purposeful. Chassis fans? Loud enough to hum the song of uptime. Every port, every slot, every airflow vent whispered, "*I process more in one second than your laptop dreams of in a week.*" This was **form married to function**.

4. The modularity was unmatched. You could scale I/O, processing, and encryption horsepower **independently**. With a mix of **40GbE, 10GbE, and copper ports**, it played nice with legacy infrastructure and **went toe-to-toe with modern hyperscale needs**. Want to migrate from MPLS to EVPN? Easy. Just re-slot your cards, update your config, and let the SRX5400 **shuriken its way into the future.**

5. JunOS remained the soul of the system—calm, logical, and hierarchically beautiful. The CLI welcomed seasoned warriors and offered fair warnings to newbies. Committing configuration on the SRX5400 wasn't just a routine—it was a **ceremony**. You didn't write policies. You inscribed them like sutras onto the blade of your network security strategy.

6. With **dedicated control planes** and **separated data paths**, the SRX5400 ensured that even under duress—like a flood of DDoS packets or a massive application rollout—it kept its cool. Routing, forwarding, and flow inspection all ran in harmony. Nothing starved. Nothing dropped. Everything **executed like clockwork with a warrior's grace**.

7. Chassis clustering on the SRX5400 was textbook Juniper: Active/active HA, stateful failover, synchronized sessions, fabric interfaces that refused to flinch. You could knock out half a node, and your services wouldn't even blink. It wasn't redundancy—it was **resilience forged in silicon.**

8. AppSecure? Weaponized. With multiple SPCs, the SRX5400 ran **AppTrack, AppFW, AppQoS**, and even **AppID logging** across thousands of flows without skipping a beat. This wasn't DPI for the sake of compliance. This was **application-centric traffic judo**, designed to tame everything from Salesforce to Slack to obscure P2P traffic hidden in HTTP headers.

9. IDP wasn't just enabled—it was *unleashed*. Full signature coverage, granular policy profiles, custom rule deployment, and real-time packet intervention. With SPCs dedicated to nothing but security, you could detect, analyze, and block multi-vector threats in real time. This was **an IDS dojo with packet drop privileges.**

10. VPN handling was absurdly good. Thousands of **IPsec tunnels**, hardware crypto offload, dynamic re-keying, and seamless integration with external authentication servers. The SRX5400 could become the **central hub for encrypted connectivity across continents**, all while logging and inspecting encrypted flows with the precision of a digital scalpel.

11. Logging? Think **network haiku with context**. Each alert was timestamped, categorized, zone-tagged, and detailed with flow metadata. Your SIEM didn't just get data—it got **wisdom**. Alerts weren't noise. They were **signal amplified through structure**.

12. Deployment flexibility gave the 5400 serious versatility. DMZ core? Done. ISP peering point with BGP and inline threat detection? Easy. East-west segmentation inside a hybrid cloud spine? No problem. You didn't adapt your network to the SRX5400. It **adapted to your vision**.

13. And it didn't complain. Throw 100 VLANs, NAT policies, QoS rules, and flow mirroring at it —and it said, "Cool. Got anything harder?"

14. It even made **regulatory compliance bearable**. PCI-DSS, HIPAA, NERC, ISO—you name it. The SRX5400 let you slice logs, generate audit trails, and write policies so precise you could **hand them to an auditor like they were recipe cards**. And if the auditor asked for proof? You showed them the logs. And the firewall smiled.

15. High-performance networking was just the beginning. The 5400 also ran **CoS, traffic shaping, route filtering**, and full **BGP/MPLS/VPLS/EVPN support**, meaning it could *also* double as a tier-one edge router *and* a threat detection system. Because why not? Samurai don't specialize. They **master.**

16. If you were feeling brave, the SRX5400 was perfect for **automation ninjutsu**. Push configs via Ansible. Query policies via REST. Validate sessions using Junos PyEZ. You didn't just configure it. You **orchestrated it like a conductor at a cyberpunk symphony.**

17. Was it perfect? No. It ran hot. It required real planning for airflow and cable discipline. It didn't suffer fools lightly. But that's what made it **real infrastructure**. It demanded competence. And rewarded it with **absolute control**.

18. Admins who wielded the SRX5400 weren't just engineers. They were **guardians of the core**, trusted to make split-second decisions that determined the security posture of entire enterprises. You didn't just rack a 5400. You **installed peace of mind**.

19. In deployment stories across the globe, SRX5400s handled **massive policy loads, complex NAT scenarios, and terabit-scale flow records** without cracking. As long as you respected the config tree, the box **never broke faith.**

20. For many orgs, it was the **last firewall they ever had to think about**. It simply did its job, week after week, logging, inspecting, dropping, and passing with samurai discipline. Firmware updates were like tea ceremonies: rare, intentional, and always worthy of reverence.

21. When newer cloud-native models started emerging with web UIs and AI-driven dashboards, the SRX5400 remained steadfast. No fluff. No bloat. Just **throughput, policies, and purpose.**

22. And it was beautiful. Not in the sleek, touchscreen way. But in the **"machine-that-defends-your-digital-honor" kind of way.** You could hear its fans, feel its heat, and know your packets were protected by something built to last.

23. Even as newer SRX5K siblings stepped up, the 5400 remained **the katana that forged the way**. Quiet, deadly, and precise. You didn't retire it. You upgraded around it. And let it keep doing what it did best: **everything.**

24. So here's to the **SRX5400**: the Core Network Katana. The box that reminded us that defense isn't about blinking lights and dashboards. It's about strength, balance, clarity, and the occasional `run clear security flow`.

Chapter 16: SRX5600 – The Colossus with Custom Cards

1. The **SRX5600** didn't just enter the datacenter—it reshaped it with the elegance of a bulldozer and the precision of a brain surgeon. As the **middle child of the SRX5K series**, it blended maximum performance with modular freedom, giving admins the power to customize for any scenario without needing a forklift upgrade every six months. Whether you needed high-speed inspection, deep segmentation, or enough crypto horsepower to rival a government black site, the 5600 was ready. With up to **960 Gbps of firewall throughput** and a scalable architecture of **12 midplane slots**, it was less of a firewall and more of a **network engine wrapped in reinforced steel**. Every slot was a decision. Every configuration was a declaration of control. The SRX5600 wasn't a purchase—it was an **infrastructure philosophy**.

2. Physically, the 5600 was a **17U behemoth**, demanding its own zip code inside the rack. But for that space, you got **insane I/O density**, modular SPC/NPC combinations, and enough airflow control to avoid turning your datacenter into a wind tunnel. With **2 Tbps of backplane capacity**, this thing could reroute, inspect, and crush traffic from thousands of clients without breaking a sweat. It didn't just manage bandwidth—it absorbed it, tamed it, and routed it like a cybernetic samurai. And thanks to redundant control planes and power supplies, failure wasn't part of its vocabulary. You didn't install the SRX5600 to keep up — you installed it to **take over**.

3. The key to the SRX5600's power was its **customizable internals**. Each of its 12 slots could be populated with NPCs for flow and I/O handling or SPCs for inspection and security services. This made it a living machine — adaptable to edge deployments, core routing, inline security, or even multi-tenant virtualized environments. Want to run full-blown IDP across dozens of 10GbE links? Load up on SPCs. Need fast packet forwarding and stateless inspection for a BGP-heavy edge? Stack NPCs and let it roar. This was more than configuration. It was **tailored packet supremacy**.

4. Unsurprisingly, **JunOS** remained the command center of this digital fortress. The familiar CLI hierarchy allowed admins to traverse vast policy trees, build NAT rules, enforce security zones, and script automation without missing a beat. And the addition of **logical systems** allowed true multi-tenant deployment, slicing the chassis into independently managed virtual firewalls. It wasn't just one SRX — it could be **a dozen firewalls in a trench coat**, each with isolated interfaces and policies. This made the 5600 a favorite in service provider and government spaces. No fluff. Just **deep, deliberate segmentation and security**.

5. When it came to **IDP**, the SRX5600 was practically clairvoyant. You could enable multiple detection engines, apply them per zone or interface, and filter out the noise with rule categories more organized than your last three apartment moves. STRIKE signature feeds flowed into it like training manuals for packet ninjas. And unlike smaller boxes, the 5600 didn't stutter under full-scale inspection — it analyzed, logged, and acted without delay. It could catch low-and-slow attacks, polymorphic exploits, and even application-layer shenanigans like protocol tunneling or suspicious DNS queries. IDP wasn't a feature here. It was **a way of life**.

6. AppSecure elevated traffic visibility to divine levels. With enough SPCs in play, AppTrack could fingerprint applications mid-flow without dropping throughput, while AppFW enforced behavioral restrictions like a traffic cop with a black belt. AppQoS let you prioritize mission-critical flows, throttle bandwidth hogs, and shape traffic with absolute authority. With AppID, you weren't guessing — you were **pinpointing**. It could detect evasive protocols, encrypted applications, and weird payload patterns in real time. And the logs? Beautiful, detailed, timestamped declarations of **network sovereignty**. With AppSecure, the SRX5600 didn't watch traffic — it **read its mind**.

7. VPN performance on the SRX5600 was off the charts. With hardware-accelerated crypto processing, you could terminate **tens of thousands of tunnels** simultaneously without sweating latency or jitter. Remote sites, third-party access, user VPNs, site-to-site, IKEv1/v2 — it handled them all like a bouncer memorizing names at the velvet rope. Route-based or policy-based? Doesn't matter. The 5600 let you design your tunnel architecture without compromise. And the tunnel diagnostics? Crystal clear. You didn't troubleshoot here. You **verified success**.

8. High availability on the SRX5600 was practically divine. Active/active clustering, session synchronization, fabric link redundancy, and multiple control planes meant you could rip a PSU out mid-traffic and the box wouldn't blink. Cluster failover could happen in milliseconds, and session state survived just about everything except typos in your `set security` `policies` line. Fabric links tied nodes together like blood oaths, keeping flows alive even during firmware upgrades or unplanned outages. This wasn't just uptime. It was **eternal vigilance as a service**.

9. Logging on the SRX5600 was more than an operational necessity—it was an **audit-grade epic**. Every session was chronicled, every NAT decision noted, every signature match logged with enough context to reconstruct an incident from scratch. Export logs to SIEMs, syslog collectors, or Juniper Security Director with ease. Or dig into them locally with grep-fu and Jedi-like CLI skills. Either way, you didn't guess. You **knew**. And when the breach review meeting started, your SRX logs spoke like a **seasoned witness**.

10. Performance tuning turned into an **art form**. With dozens of tweakable knobs, from flow control to inspection depth to session limits and buffer profiles, the SRX5600 invited you to **master its rhythm**. And when tuned right, it danced—flowing multi-gig traffic across zones, dropping garbage, enforcing trust, and reporting it all back in real time. Most boxes just tried to keep up with load. The SRX5600 choreographed it. Like a firewall ballet, if the ballet involved **blocking port scans with shurikens**.

11. Automation? It welcomed it with open RPCs. NETCONF, REST API, Python, PyEZ—you could orchestrate a full config push, run event-driven responses, and validate policy compliance without touching a console. Ansible? Yes. Salt? Sure. You didn't need a GUI—you needed **intent-driven execution**. And this firewall delivered it like a disciplined agent awaiting orders.

12. Flexibility was key. DMZ core? Absolutely. Segmented multitenant services? Built for it. East-west firewalling in a cloud-spanning edge? Already there. The SRX5600 adapted to roles with the grace of a shapeshifter—high-throughput guardian, VPN hub, IDP sentinel, AppID gatekeeper. It didn't ask "can I?" It asked **"what else?"**

13. And then there was the **community respect**. Anyone who had deployed, tuned, or survived a full config audit with an SRX5600 walked a little taller. This box didn't babysit. It **demanded understanding**. And when you gave it that? It protected your infrastructure like a lion with a mission.

14. Its quirks were few but present. Large configs could feel like they needed a config whisperer. Boot times could test your patience. Module compatibility occasionally needed double-checking. But if those were the trade-offs for **a fortress that never sleeps**, most admins gladly paid them.

15. In many deployments, the SRX5600 became **a linchpin**. Not one firewall among many, but the backbone—the critical guardian where all traffic met, where all threats were analyzed, and where uptime wasn't just desired—it was **mandatory**.

16. The sound of it running was a chorus of fans and focus. You could walk into a server room and know which rack housed the SRX5600 just by the way the air moved. It didn't hum. It *hummed with purpose*. The airflow was calculated. The architecture was intentional. This wasn't hardware. It was **ritualized readiness**.

17. Uptime on these units became legendary. Years without fail. Policy pushes during business hours. Firmware upgrades with zero interruption. This was a box that ran through floods, power surges, configuration flubs, and at least one time someone accidentally vacuumed the power strip. And it **kept going**.

18. In security briefings, you didn't say "we think our firewall caught it." You said, "The SRX5600 flagged, dropped, and logged the threat by 13:52. Please see line 1287 of the event logs." That wasn't confidence. That was **authority**.

19. Even as the next-gen SRX platforms entered the fray with more cloud integrations, GUI dashboards, and fluff, the 5600 remained the **operator's firewall**. Built to command line. Tuned for performance. **Respected in every rack it lived in**.

20. Teams who deployed them didn't just rack them—they **defended with them**. There was pride in the syntax. Pride in the logs. And pride in knowing that even at 80% capacity, this firewall was just stretching.

21. Eventually, newer models took the spotlight. The 5800. The 5400 with higher-density cards. And yet, many SRX5600s remain in service today—faithful, formidable, and still pulling security duty like a grizzled sensei.

22. You don't decommission an SRX5600 casually. You decommission it with respect, export its config, and maybe send it to a lab where it trains the next generation of packet warriors. It's not end-of-life. It's **legend-in-retirement**.

23. So here's to the SRX5600: the Colossus with Custom Cards. The firewall that scaled, trained, protected, and never asked for more than clean power and sharp policy syntax. When it blocked a packet, it didn't log it—it **honored the process**.

24. You didn't just learn JunOS on this box. You learned how to firewall for real. And when you got promoted, it was partly because you spoke fluent SRX5600.

25. Next up: **Chapter 17 – SRX5800: The Summit of Stateful Security**. Bring a config backup and a headband. It's time for the final form.

Chapter 17: SRX5800 – The Alpha Predator

1. The **SRX5800** is the firewall equivalent of an apex predator—ruthless, powerful, and utterly dominant at the top of the security food chain. When Juniper built this beast, they didn't ask what a firewall should do. They asked what *nothing else* could do, and then made sure the SRX5800 could handle it. Whether you needed to process **over 2 Tbps of firewall throughput**, scale to **millions of concurrent sessions,** or survive an attack that melted lesser boxes, the SRX5800 was ready. Ready to scan. Ready to route. Ready to enforce policy with the kind of decisive confidence typically reserved for ancient deities and elite martial artists. This wasn't infrastructure. This was **network sovereignty embodied in a 16U chassis**.

2. The SRX5800 doesn't whisper its capabilities—it roars them through **14 midplane slots** and a backplane built to laugh in the face of DDoS attacks. Each chassis can be packed with a high-octane mix of **SPCs and NPCs**, delivering custom-built performance aligned with your network's specific demands. You want a perimeter guardian? Done. An internal traffic slicer, threat hunter, and VPN mega-hub? Easy. This firewall doesn't bend to roles. It **redefines them**. And when you hear the whir of its fans spin up, you know something serious is about to be filtered.

3. Where the 5400 and 5600 offered precision and modularity, the 5800 delivers **blunt-force elegance**. It has the scale to protect governments, multinational corporations, and critical infrastructure simultaneously. And because it supports **tens of millions of concurrent sessions**, you could run the digital operations of a small nation through it and still have room for your QA team to run vulnerability scans. The box is big. The logs are bigger. And the confidence it inspires in those who manage it? **Immeasurable.**

4. JunOS on the SRX5800 is the same spiritual discipline as on its smaller siblings, but at scale, it transforms from structured CLI to **mission-critical syntax scripture**. One misstep can reroute gigabits of traffic. One flawless policy line can safeguard a datacenter from a zero-day blitz. Every `commit confirmed` feels like lighting a beacon of intent, and every `show security flow session` reads like the operational log of a spaceship in the middle of a battle. This isn't just configuration. It's **cyber-defense choreography**. And you're the firewall samurai calling the moves.

5. Its support for **logical systems** is unparalleled. You can carve the 5800 into **multiple independent virtual firewalls**, each with isolated routing, security zones, management, and services. That makes it a perfect fit for multitenant environments, ISPs, and service providers who don't just need separation—they need **true operational autonomy within a single device**. And when those tenants hit gigabit+ speeds, the 5800 doesn't flinch. It just allocates the flows and continues hunting threats. It's the one firewall you can treat like a network slice generator without compromise.

6. AppSecure shines like never before on this box. It identifies and classifies thousands of applications in real-time, across massive bandwidth streams, and can enforce QoS, rate limits, and signature-based blocks with zero user impact. You want to slow down TikTok but give Salesforce full throttle? It's a line of config away. Want to detect embedded VPNs, tunneled payloads, or odd TLS headers? It already has. And with AppTrack and AppFW feeding detailed logs into your SIEM, you don't just *see* your traffic. You **understand its motives**.

7. The **IDP engine** on the SRX5800 is not an add-on—it is **a surgical threat-slicing machine**. It scans at wire speed, applies custom signatures, tracks attack behavior, and executes mitigation policies like a military-grade AI with a grudge. You can detect protocol anomalies, flood behavior, advanced evasion techniques, and zero-day-style patterns without sacrificing a single packet per second of throughput. Want to deploy custom signatures based on recent threat intel?

It handles that like a private intelligence agency. The logs that come out of IDP events aren't alerts—they're **crime scene reconstructions**. And with threat feeds updating dynamically, the 5800 never sleeps.

8. VPN handling on the 5800 is **nothing short of legendary**. It supports hardware acceleration across thousands of concurrent IPsec tunnels, route-based overlays, and policy-enforced phase transitions like a cross-continental ninja highway system. Remote users? Routed. Partner interconnects? Encrypted. Geo-redundant DR links? Tunneled and protected. You could build a **global IPsec backbone** across this box and still have room to run a packet capture. The SRX5800 doesn't just handle VPNs. It **weaponizes them.**

9. High availability on the 5800 isn't optional—it's foundational. With full support for **chassis clustering**, you can build mirrored pairs with synchronized sessions, failover control, and event-resilient processing that laughs in the face of outages. Hardware swaps? Seamless. Control plane crashes? Recovered instantly. It's not just about uptime. It's about **unshakeable mission assurance**. Even if half the box falls off the rack, the other half keeps blocking threats.

10. Monitoring and log export are elevated into an art form. Every policy match, threat signature hit, flow creation, NAT rule invocation, and VPN event is **timestamped, tagged, and transmitted with forensic precision**. Junos Space Security Director, Splunk, Elastic, Graylog— you name it, the 5800 feeds them. But even local inspection using CLI is a masterclass in operational clarity. You don't need filters. You just need to **follow the flows**. And in a post-incident debrief, no one questions the SRX5800's version of events. It's **the firewall of record**.

11. Automation was baked into its bones. API-driven control, RPC access, and scripting hooks across every subsystem make it an orchestration dream. Whether you're pushing Ansible playbooks, automating config audits with Python, or building on-demand VPN provisioning from a portal, the SRX5800 **executes like a digital samurai under a DevOps flag**. You don't just automate with this box. You **conduct infrastructure** like a security composer.

12. Flexibility is where the 5800 truly earns its apex title. It can live at the data center edge, deep in the core, serving as a service provider node or as a full-blown SDN-integrated inline security engine. One day it's filtering per-user sessions on a university campus. The next, it's running deep inspection for a high-frequency trading firm. Whatever the role, it dominates it. The SRX5800 doesn't just adjust. It **ascends.**

13. The respect it commands from the community is unmatched. Admins speak about the 5800 the way pilots speak about fighter jets: with awe, respect, and the occasional war story about reboots, configs, or midnight policy pushes during ransomware outbreaks. If you've tuned one, maintained one, or survived an outage and recovered one, you don't forget it. You **earn a badge**. And in return, it never lets you down.

14. Of course, it comes with expectations. The learning curve is Everest with a CLI prompt. The documentation reads like an epic. But for those who invest the time, the 5800 **pays back with protection, predictability, and power**. If you want easy, look elsewhere. If you want elite, start racking.

15. Some of the longest uptimes in the field have been seen on SRX5800s. It's not uncommon to find units running for **five years uninterrupted**, defending banks, airports, research institutions, and even military installations without complaint. Updates were done with precision. Power cycling was ceremonial. And day-to-day operations were as stable as stone. Because it wasn't just built to run. It was built to **endure**.

16. Even when newer cloud-native firewalls promised speed and UI, none matched the **raw field dominance** of a tuned 5800. It didn't just block. It **judged**. It contextualized. It enforced layered policy like a tiered monastery of security monks with blades. While others looked sleek, the 5800 looked you in the eye and asked if you were *ready*. Most weren't.

17. Its replacement cycle wasn't triggered by weakness, but by **organizational change**. Businesses moved to containers. Workloads scattered across clouds. But in hybrid cores and trusted zones, the 5800 still **patrolled with purpose**. You didn't retire it. You honored it.

18. Stories abound of 5800s catching insider threats, rogue contractors, exfiltration attempts, and misrouted BGP advertisements before the rest of the infrastructure even flinched. It wasn't flashy. It just **knew what didn't belong**. And it acted. With logs, with alerts, with blocklists. With certainty.

19. For security architects, the 5800 wasn't a choice. It was a **final form**. Something to build around. Something to trust. And something to inspire.

20. You can always spot a seasoned admin who's worked with a 5800. They don't panic. They grep with confidence. They handle policy like swordplay. And when others gasp at packet storms, they just nod and say, *"Let the 5800 handle it."*

21. It took up space, sure. But every inch of that rack was **earned**. It didn't waste power. It turned it into **defensive clarity**. It didn't crave attention. It *commanded obedience* from every flow that passed through.

22. Many remain in service to this day, tucked into hardened cages, scanning critical sectors and **shielding digital civilization**. They are not quaint. They are not legacy. They are **living guardians**, still sharp, still fast, still deadly.

23. The SRX5800 was more than the sum of its SPCs and NPCs. It was a firewall that gave security engineers **peace of mind**, even in chaos. And when the noise came, it listened carefully and then cut straight through.

24. So here's to the **SRX5800**: The Alpha Predator. Built not just to compete, but to **dominate**. To protect. To endure. And to teach every admin who touched it how to be **better**.

25. Next up: **Chapter 18 – SRX300: Leaner, Meaner, and Made for Modern Branches**. Let's scale back and rediscover elegance in small form.

Chapter 18: vSRX – The Virtual Ninja in the Cloud Scrolls

1. The **vSRX** is the Juniper firewall that traded steel chassis for software agility, bringing the soul of a samurai into the realm of virtualization. It didn't need a rack. It didn't need airflow. It needed only hypervisors, cloud APIs, and a mission. Designed to run on KVM, VMware, OpenStack, AWS, Azure, and just about anything else you can acronym, the vSRX brought **stateful security and rich features into virtual form**. It's not watered down. It's not junior. It's a **fully armed ninja wrapped in a .qcow2 cloak**. The cloud didn't see it coming—and that's exactly the point.

2. Think of vSRX as a spiritual clone of the SRX physical models—complete with **AppSecure, IDP, IPsec VPN, NAT, and advanced routing**—but tuned for lightweight, elastic environments. It spins up in seconds, integrates with orchestration tools, and scales horizontally faster than your compliance team can schedule a review. You can burst into new cloud zones, clone vSRXs for specific tenants, or automate defense with Terraform, Ansible, or native APIs. Each vSRX instance carries the DNA of JunOS, giving you consistent CLI and management regardless of where it lives. It's the same syntax. The same logic. Just **unbound by hardware**.

3. Performance, of course, is relative to the environment. But given enough vCPUs and memory, vSRX can deliver **multi-gig throughput**, thousands of sessions, and full-featured inspection across tunnels, zones, and interfaces. On-prem? No problem. In the cloud? Already protecting. In a hybrid overlay with SD-WAN? Happily. This isn't an emulated test box. It's **a real firewall on a metaphysical diet**.

4. And yes—it still runs **AppSecure**. Application tracking, firewalling, QoS tagging, and detection analytics are all on board, ready to sniff out Spotify in your corporate VPC like a bloodhound. Whether it's in Kubernetes or next to your cloud ERP, the vSRX understands application behavior and enforces policy like it's **guarding digital treasure**. Want per-user application control in AWS? Easy. Want real-time logging into CloudWatch, Elastic, or Security Director? It's already set up. The vSRX brings **next-gen traffic wisdom to virtual borders**.

5. Intrusion detection and prevention don't disappear either. The vSRX supports **IDP with real-time signatures from the STRIKE feed**, custom rule sets, and zone-based enforcement. You can detect lateral movement in a cloud subnet. Stop malformed packets before they touch storage. Or watch for tunneling attempts from infected containers. It doesn't just protect. It **watches for intent**.

6. The real power of vSRX lies in its **automation superpowers**. Spin up with Terraform. Push policy with Ansible. Validate flow behavior using REST APIs. It fits seamlessly into CI/CD pipelines, security-as-code strategies, and ephemeral architectures where your security perimeter lives and dies by YAML. There's no click fatigue. There's just **declarative defense**. And the vSRX speaks the language fluently.

7. VPNs? Still here. You can deploy **IPsec tunnels, dynamic peer profiles, BGP over IPsec, and even GRE encapsulation**, all inside a cloud-native VM. The vSRX acts as a branch hub, a remote site connector, or a secure endpoint for third-party integrations. Tunnels form quickly. Logs remain detailed. You don't sacrifice functionality for portability. You just **gain flexibility**.

8. From a cost and licensing standpoint, the vSRX brings options. Juniper offers consumption models ranging from **throughput-based subscriptions to instance-hour billing**, perfect for dynamic cloud environments. You can license features individually or as bundles, integrate with service provider billing platforms, or go full marketplace mode on AWS or Azure. You control the spend. You scale as needed. And you **deploy security like code**.

9. Logging is fully intact and incredibly versatile. You can forward to syslog, stream via telemetry, or dump logs into cloud-native tools for compliance and alerting. vSRX doesn't hide anything. It **tells the truth in structured, timestamped, JSON-fed detail**. Whether you're chasing compliance, debugging a misrouted flow, or explaining to a dev why their container was quarantined, the logs back you up.

10. The real magic is in how **vSRX bridges traditional and modern IT**. You can run one in a legacy VMware cluster protecting an old ERP system, and another inside Azure filtering traffic to your Kubernetes ingress controller. Same policy structure. Same enforcement logic. Total environmental awareness. The vSRX is **security transcendence in a bootable ISO**.

11. When used in tandem with Juniper's **Contrail or Security Director Cloud**, the vSRX becomes part of a **broader, orchestrated fabric**. You can push policy globally, receive telemetry instantly, and enforce microsegmentation without lifting your hands off the keyboard. It's no longer about devices. It's about **distributed intent**. And that's where vSRX shines.

12. High availability in cloud? Absolutely. Deploy pairs. Use auto-scaling groups. Drop in some routing and session sync, and you're ready for failover across zones, regions, or even continents. No downtime. No drama. Just **resilient cloud fortification**.

13. And while it doesn't have a chassis, the vSRX has **just as much heart**. It's where performance meets portability. Where legacy power meets dev-friendly packaging. Where JunOS proves it can still thrive in the age of containers and APIs. The vSRX doesn't pretend to be physical. It **transcends it**.

14. Engineers who master the vSRX gain an edge. They speak both CLI and cloud-native dialects. They understand how to scale security horizontally, define it as code, and adapt it to platforms with constantly shifting boundaries. You can't scare them with a new region, a new orchestrator, or a new threat model. Because they **think like vSRX fights** — fast, efficient, adaptive.

15. The vSRX may not blink, whir, or take up rack space. But it still protects with the same intensity and intuition as its steel-bodied ancestors. It is a whisper in the hypervisor. A blade in the overlay. A **ninja in the cloud scrolls**.

16. So here's to the vSRX: proof that firewalls didn't die in the cloud—they evolved. They virtualized. They adapted. And they came back more agile, more intelligent, and more dangerous than ever. Whether you're defending an EC2 subnet or guarding a multi-tenant K8s stack, this ninja's ready. You spin it up, feed it policy, and watch as it **silently dominates**.

17. The vSRX also redefines what it means to **scale security horizontally**. Instead of relying on massive hardware footprints, you simply **spin up more firewalls**—each with their own interface sets, policies, and inspection logic. Load balancing becomes automatic, redundancy is built into the cloud platform, and resource elasticity turns traffic spikes into opportunities, not outages. No bottlenecks. No forklift upgrades. Just **smooth, incremental expansion** with a ninja's efficiency. It's not just a firewall—it's a fluid, shape-shifting line of defense.

18. Its portability makes it a top choice for **disaster recovery scenarios**, too. Got a backup VPC ready to go? Drop a vSRX in there, sync your policies, and you've got a mirrored security posture without touching a single physical cable. Failover between regions or availability zones is as fast as your routing table allows. And restoring full functionality doesn't require racking and stacking—it requires an image and a config. Simplicity, thy name is **vSRX**.

19. And let's talk multi-cloud. The vSRX doesn't care whether it's protecting AWS, Azure, GCP, or some Kubernetes sandbox on a Raspberry Pi cluster—it treats them all as fair game. Unified policies mean fewer inconsistencies. Federated telemetry brings centralized insight. And cloud-native deployment methods keep infrastructure-as-code teams happy. It's **multi-cloud security without multiverse confusion**.

20. In proof-of-concept labs, the vSRX often **outperforms expectations**. Admins expect a lightweight edge device and get an **application-aware threat hunter**. It handles full routing stacks, supports OSPF, BGP, static, multicast, and even segment routing, if you dare. Developers stop seeing firewalls as obstacles and start seeing them as programmable gatekeepers. Compliance teams love the audit trails. And security teams love **having eyes everywhere**.

21. Training on vSRX is also more accessible than ever. Spin up lab instances. Break things safely. Snapshot your failures, roll back, and learn the flow logic in ways you can't with hardware. It's how new engineers build confidence before working on production SRX boxes. And it's how experienced engineers **refine their cloud skills without risk**. This is a dojo in a hypervisor.

22. It also brings legacy networks **into the modern fold**. You can build tunnels from your ancient MPLS edge to your shiny S3 buckets with firewall enforcement along the way. You don't have to rebuild everything. Just deploy smartly. Let the vSRX bridge the gap. **It speaks both dialects.**

23. Even when the world shifts to microservices and AI workloads, there will always be a need for visibility, control, and safe egress. That's where vSRX lives—not as a relic, but as a native protector in a chaotic realm. It doesn't fear change. It thrives in it. And wherever packets go next, the **virtual ninja will be waiting**.

24. The next time someone asks if firewalls belong in the cloud, you'll have a better answer: **they don't just belong—they flourish**. And when that firewall is the vSRX, you'll also have the logs, tunnels, policies, and analytics to prove it. It's small. It's fast. It's everywhere. And it **knows your apps better than you do**.

25. Next up: **Chapter 19 – SRX320: Compact. Tactical. Effective.** From cloud ninjas to physical warriors, let's meet the field unit that guards small offices with serious bite.

Chapter 19: cSRX – Container Combat Unit

1. If the vSRX is a ninja, then the **cSRX** is its minimalist cousin: leaner, faster, and containerized for war in the **microservice trenches**. The cSRX doesn't come with a chassis, fans, or boot BIOS—just Docker compatibility and JunOS stripped to the bare essentials. Built for **Kubernetes, Docker, and container-based infrastructures**, it was designed to **spin up fast, scale sideways, and protect at light speed**. You won't find blinking lights or rack screws here—just **YAML, kubectl, and the unmistakable scent of DevSecOps in motion**. When containers call for security that lives and breathes at their pace, the cSRX responds without hesitation. It's not about bulk. It's about **precision in milliseconds**.

2. The cSRX lives inside container pods, running as a lightweight JunOS instance, stripped down and tuned for dynamic environments. Its focus is crystal clear: **layered security for containerized apps**, with full support for **AppSecure, IDP, NAT, and session-based flow enforcement**. It works in CI/CD pipelines, drops into pods, and scales horizontally faster than your build server can blink. You can deploy it in Kubernetes via Helm or custom YAML, attach it to service meshes, or let it stand guard at the edge of your container clusters. Need east-west inspection between pods? No problem. Need virtual segmentation between services? It lives for it. The cSRX is **firewalling reimagined for the speed of containers**.

3. Unlike traditional firewalls, the cSRX is **ephemeral by design**. Spin one up to protect a job. Destroy it when the job finishes. Run them as sidecars in Kubernetes or deploy as micro-perimeters around sensitive workloads. They enforce policies with the full might of JunOS—zones, firewall rules, AppFW, and IDP included. Yet they remain **stateless in lifespan**, stateful in inspection. It's a paradox that only a containerized firewall can live comfortably within. And the cSRX wears it well.

4. Performance tuning comes down to resource allocation and orchestration. You give it CPU limits and memory constraints, and it adapts accordingly. You control which interfaces are exposed, which services are logged, and where those logs go. Within those confines, the cSRX moves like liquid—**inspecting, tagging, filtering, and vanishing** when the job is done. It doesn't live forever. But while it lives? It **controls its namespace with unwavering resolve**.

5. AppSecure still plays a starring role, offering application-aware controls even inside container meshes. You can monitor traffic per service, per container, or per port. Tag flows. Prioritize services. Or detect when someone tries to sneak a browser into a backend pod. With AppTrack,

AppQoS, and AppFW fully functional, the cSRX watches everything, understands its context, and **reacts faster than most humans can type `docker ps`**.

6. IDP? Absolutely. Despite its compact form, the cSRX supports full **intrusion detection and prevention**, including STRIKE feeds, custom signatures, and inline enforcement. It's perfect for environments where **threats evolve quickly** and traditional perimeter models don't exist. You can deploy cSRX to intercept traffic in real-time, analyze flows, and stop attackers from pivoting between pods. It doesn't care if the attack comes in HTTP, gRPC, or some weird tunnel built out of DNS queries. It just watches. And **pounces**.

7. Deployment is as DevOps-friendly as it gets. Drop it into a **Kubernetes DaemonSet**, bake it into CI/CD pipelines, launch it from Jenkins, or roll it out using GitOps tools like ArgoCD or Flux. You're not managing firewalls. You're **curating security instances like artifacts in your registry**. Each one spun up from a clean image, updated with policy templates, and booted into action within seconds. There's no drama, no licensing dongles, no half-hour reboots. Just **instant, container-native defense**.

8. Logging and telemetry keep up with the modern stack, too. Forward to ELK, Splunk, Fluentd, or your favorite observability platform. JSON logs, flow records, IDP alerts—they all show up right where your SRE team already lives. Need to audit lateral movement? It's in there. Need to prove zero-trust enforcement? It's got receipts. The cSRX speaks fluent DevSecOps, and its logs are **as readable as its enforcement is deadly**.

9. Where cSRX really shines is in **microsegmentation**. Inside a Kubernetes cluster, you can deploy multiple instances of cSRX to guard service-to-service traffic with fine-grained policies. Instead of trusting namespaces or network policies alone, the cSRX brings **deep, stateful, Layer 7 policy enforcement**. You don't just block by port—you block by intent. That's the difference between good security and great security. And when every service talks to every other service, the **container combat unit becomes your final defense**.

10. VPN? Maybe not its forte—but even here, the cSRX surprises. You can deploy lightweight **IPsec or GRE tunnels** between clusters or across namespaces. It's perfect for linking dev to prod, test to staging, or cloud to on-prem in a controlled, encrypted way. And yes, it still logs like a beast. Just smaller. **Because even little ninjas carry sharp blades**.

11. Like its vSRX cousin, the cSRX integrates into orchestration and automation beautifully. Whether you're using Terraform for infrastructure, Helm for services, or CI tools for deployments, the cSRX fits. It doesn't complain. It doesn't bloat. It just takes its config, checks its runtime, and **starts inspecting traffic with unblinking eyes**. From dev sandbox to hardened production, it moves where needed and always leaves a trail of defeated threats.

12. Don't mistake its small size for simplicity. The cSRX still requires careful policy crafting, resource planning, and orchestration design. But when done right, it enables **true DevSecOps harmony**, where developers don't fear security because it lives side by side with their services. No context switches. No manual reviews. Just **code-defined guardianship**.

13. Troubleshooting it is refreshingly modern. Logs stream via stdout. Diagnostics run from kubectl exec. And snapshots take seconds to export and analyze. You don't need rack access or console cables. You need **kubectl, a coffee, and about three grep filters**. That's all it takes to trace flows through your cloud-native battle zone.

14. In incident response, cSRX makes a perfect tactical ally. Drop it on-demand into compromised namespaces. Intercept egress from suspicious containers. Log every connection attempt like a courtroom stenographer and terminate with surgical precision. Containment becomes a code update. And **remediation is a restart away**.

15. As cloud-native continues to rise, so too does the relevance of firewalling **where containers live, breathe, and misbehave**. The cSRX doesn't try to replace the perimeter—it becomes a new kind of perimeter: ephemeral, containerized, and **coded into existence**. It's security born from velocity. Inspection without infrastructure. And **defense, delivered by image pull**.

16. So here's to the cSRX: the Container Combat Unit, the tiniest warrior with the sharpest flow inspection, the sidecar of justice in a world of ephemeral chaos. It's fast. It's quiet. And it knows the cloud better than most architects. When your pods are in peril and your services need a silent sentinel, it spins up and stands ready. No boot time. No drama. Just **combat-ready enforcement from the container realm**.

17. Just because it's small doesn't mean it lacks ambition. The cSRX is more than a micro-firewall—it's a **mission-adaptive operator** inside your container cluster. Its agility allows it to respond to policy changes, load conditions, and new deployments with split-second efficiency. There's no waiting on ticketing systems or change reviews. The pipeline moves fast—and so does your security perimeter. In a world where services die and rebirth in minutes, the cSRX is there to **watch every resurrection**.

18. The cSRX thrives on impermanence. It doesn't expect uptime medals or legacy treatment—it wants to be **destroyed, recreated, and tested again**. This ephemeral nature makes it ideal for blue-green deployments, canary testing, and distributed edge enforcement. While traditional firewalls chase durability, the cSRX chases **renewal and replication**. It earns your trust not through long life, but through repeatable performance. If it goes down, another takes its place. And that is the beauty of container combat.

19. This unit is perfect for **multi-tenant architectures**, giving each team or service its own scoped security perimeter. You no longer have to convince a shared firewall to respect tenancy boundaries—you can deploy one per tenant and **enforce policy with surgical precision**. Billing becomes easier. Isolation becomes stronger. And developers feel empowered, not obstructed. The cSRX isn't just security-as-code—it's **security-within-code**.

20. Observability is another core strength. Unlike black-box firewalls, the cSRX emits logs designed for structured consumption. Your Prometheus, Grafana, or Datadog stack won't have to guess what happened—the logs tell the whole tale in plain JSON. You'll see threat ID, timestamp, flow path, policy action, and more. Debugging isn't just easier—it's empowering. When a threat arises, the cSRX ensures **there's a record, a reason, and a resolution path**.

21. Future-forward teams are beginning to explore **AI-assisted response mechanisms**, and the cSRX fits right in. You can wire its logs into automated SOAR pipelines, machine-learning classifiers, or feedback loops that adapt policies based on actual attack behavior. Your infrastructure reacts. Learns. Grows more defensive every time it's challenged. And the cSRX, ever patient, continues executing policy **with monk-like consistency**.

22. When used as a security building block, the cSRX doesn't just secure infrastructure — it teaches **architectural discipline**. You begin to segment services intentionally. You place security at ingress, egress, and interconnect. You start viewing your architecture not just as a set of workloads, but as **a battlefield**, where each node has defense, purpose, and policy.

23. Eventually, you realize this little container has given your team a superpower. Not just visibility or enforcement — but **resilience at scale**. It's no longer about pushing patches or scaling hardware. It's about spinning defense into your pipeline like unit tests and deployment keys. It's about making security **automatic and ambient**. That's the quiet revolution of the cSRX.

24. So whether you're deploying 50 microservices, defending Kubernetes ingress, or just getting started with cloud-native defense, remember: there's a combat unit that fits inside a container and hits like a heavyweight. It's portable, it's policy-driven, and it's been through more CI pipelines than your favorite dev tools. That's not hype — that's heritage. Juniper brought decades of firewalling to bear inside a single Docker image. And now, it's **ready to run for your pods.**

Chapter 20: Advanced Threat Protection – Juniper's Ninja Stars

1. In the dojo of cybersecurity, Juniper's **Advanced Threat Protection (ATP)** isn't just a product — it's an **arsenal of ninja stars**, forged to track, analyze, and eliminate stealthy threats with precision. While firewalls block and log, ATP hunts, learns, and **fights back**. It doesn't wait for known signatures — it detects behavior, dissects payloads, and deploys intelligence at network speed. Where traditional defenses say, "stop what I know," ATP whispers, "I'll find what you've never seen." It's Juniper's answer to evasive malware, lateral movement, and zero-day exploits that think they're clever. In short: it's the difference between defense and **counterattack**. And every packet is a potential sparring partner.

2. ATP in the Juniper universe is a **cloud-delivered, constantly-evolving threat detection suite**. It integrates with SRX firewalls — physical, virtual, and containerized — to offer **inline detection, post-delivery analysis, and real-time threat intel**. The engine uses multiple layers: **static analysis, dynamic sandboxing, and machine learning** to classify files, inspect URLs, and profile behavior. This isn't a black box of magic — it's a dojo of techniques, each with a purpose. You don't just block suspicious traffic — you **study it, profile it, and prepare for its cousins**. ATP makes your firewall not just a gatekeeper, but a **sensei of security**.

3. The cornerstone of ATP is **Sky ATP**, Juniper's cloud-based brain that absorbs threat intelligence from global sources and distributes it to your SRX in near real-time. Think of it as a digital informant network, constantly collecting data on malware, botnets, command-and-control infrastructure, and zero-day behaviors. When your firewall sees a suspicious file or session, it can forward metadata—or the full payload—to Sky ATP for examination. Static checks run hashes, look for known indicators, and match against cloud databases. Then, if needed, the file is sandboxed, detonated, and **interrogated like a digital shinobi**. If the file misbehaves, it gets flagged. If not, it's logged and forgotten like a defeated novice.

4. Sky ATP doesn't just detect threats—it learns from them. If malware tries to obfuscate itself, evade detection, or escalate privileges, Sky ATP **watches, remembers, and records** every action. Then it updates your firewalls with verdicts: malicious, benign, or suspicious. This verdict feeds into firewall policies, triggering actions like drop, quarantine, alert, or share with SIEMs. But here's the kicker—ATP shares back across your organization, so the next site, user, or data center is already defended. You don't just detect once—you **defend everywhere**. ATP builds a memory palace of malware and **locks every future door**.

5. ATP's effectiveness lies in its **layered detection strategy**. Static analysis is the first swipe—quick, efficient, and designed to catch known badness. Dynamic analysis is the second move—deep inspection using sandboxes that simulate victim machines. Machine learning is the third strike—pattern recognition built from global behavior profiles. And finally, custom feeds and policy-driven logic let ATP respond to threats in a way that aligns with your organization's risk appetite. It's not one technique. It's **a choreography of layered attacks against attackers**. And ATP never blinks.

6. Integration is seamless with SRX devices—whether you're running a vSRX in AWS, an SRX5800 in a data center, or a cSRX in Kubernetes. Once connected, the firewall begins feeding samples and requesting verdicts. Policy rules can reference these verdicts using **custom security intelligence match conditions**, allowing you to block IPs, domains, files, or even behaviors dynamically. It's plug-and-hunt simplicity. With every log line, ATP grows smarter. And your network becomes **less of a target and more of a trap**.

7. Don't forget about **SSL inspection**—because encrypted threats are no longer edge cases. ATP integrates with SRX SSL decryption to analyze payloads **even when they're wrapped in TLS armor**. Files can be unpacked, scanned, and re-wrapped mid-flight without impacting legitimate traffic. It's like intercepting a scroll, reading it, and resealing it before the enemy notices. The attacker thinks they're safe. ATP says, **"Not in my dojo."**

8. Threat scoring and analytics are beautifully built into ATP's interface and telemetry feeds. You don't just see alerts—you get **rich context**, showing kill chains, attack vectors, and behavior trails. It maps the threat lifecycle, from delivery to execution to command-and-control attempts. You see who was targeted, what they downloaded, and what the malware did in the sandbox. This isn't just reporting—it's **threat archeology with a vengeance**. You understand your adversary. And you sharpen your policy blade accordingly.

9. ATP also enables **adaptive enforcement**. Threat intel feeds can update firewall rules in real-time. Malicious URLs, IPs, and file hashes can be blocked without human intervention. You can configure your firewall to **learn from what it sees**, applying mitigation automatically. It's the closest thing to reflex in a network. You hit the attacker once—and the system **remembers forever**.

10. API access lets ATP become part of a broader SOAR or threat intelligence ecosystem. You can export IOCs, pull verdicts, query logs, or **trigger playbooks** when malicious activity is detected. It's not just reactive—it's proactive, connected, and flexible. And because it's Juniper, it integrates cleanly with **Security Director, Contrail, and even third-party orchestration platforms**. ATP doesn't need the spotlight. It just needs access. And then it **quietly turns your firewall into a threat-seeking missile**.

11. For organizations already operating in zero-trust or microsegmented environments, ATP becomes the final layer of **behavioral context and intent detection**. You don't just assume internal traffic is safe. You observe it. You profile it. You learn from it. ATP makes sure that trust is earned, not implied. Because in the modern threat landscape, the quietest enemy often sits just inside the castle walls.

12. ATP can also integrate with **endpoint and workload protection tools**, expanding its reach beyond the firewall. Metadata from hosts can enrich detection logic. Endpoints can be isolated based on ATP verdicts. And cloud workloads can be flagged or suspended mid-execution if malicious behavior is detected. You're not just stopping files—you're **disrupting campaigns**. That's ninja-level threat response.

13. Policy tuning is as granular as a throwing star's edge. You can configure ATP by file type, source zone, destination, protocol, or user. Don't want to scan ISO files? Fine. Want to quarantine suspicious PDFs from email attachments but allow known safe scripts? Easy. ATP lets you write policies like you're crafting traps: **targeted, silent, and deadly effective**.

14. ATP is built with privacy and compliance in mind, too. Files are analyzed in regional clouds or on-prem, depending on your jurisdiction and needs. Metadata anonymization, role-based access, and audit logging ensure **transparency without compromise**. You get full threat visibility without stepping outside legal or ethical lines. Even your compliance officer will nod approvingly. And when they ask for reports? **ATP delivers PDFs with footnotes, timelines, and threat verdicts**.

15. In training and simulation environments, ATP can act like a sparring partner. You can test malware samples, run attack chains, or simulate phishing campaigns to see how ATP responds. It's not just about production defense—it's about **educating your blue team to fight better**. You learn what's blocked, what's delayed, and how fast your systems react. ATP turns your network into both fortress and classroom.

16. In the end, Juniper's Advanced Threat Protection is more than a feature. It's a philosophy. It's about looking beyond signatures, beyond logs, and beyond traffic volume. It's about asking what the packet *intends* to do. And then acting before it does. With ATP, your network doesn't just survive. It **fights back**.

17. ATP also brings threat context into focus across organizational boundaries. When one department gets hit, the intelligence spreads across the infrastructure—**turning a local response into a global immune system**. It isn't siloed knowledge—it's a rapid-fire intel distribution system. Every user benefits from every attack seen, analyzed, and remembered. This means that even junior admins reap the protection crafted by seasoned security veterans and automated ATP reactions. No knowledge hoarding. No isolated alerts. Just **network-wide defense coordination at scale**.

18. Threat attribution is another trick in ATP's arsenal. Through correlation with global feeds, threat actor profiling, and sandbox observables, ATP builds an attacker signature beyond the file. It connects behavior, source IPs, payload similarities, and campaign patterns. This allows security teams to understand not just *what* hit them, but *who* and *why*. And when you know the enemy's habits, you can build **countermeasures designed to exploit their predictability**. It's the cybersecurity equivalent of studying your rival's fighting style.

19. You can extend ATP's reach by combining it with **SecIntel**, Juniper's curated intelligence feed system. This lets you inject your own blacklists, whitelists, and custom intel into policy enforcement. ATP sees and reacts; SecIntel preloads your firewall with **specific instructions for how to respond faster**. Think of it as handing your ninja stars a target list before the battle even begins. Preemptive, efficient, and scarily effective.

20. ATP's forensic capabilities allow for powerful post-mortem insight. You can replay threat campaigns, visualize how malware behaved in the sandbox, and correlate across timelines. It's the sort of detail that turns a routine incident report into a **tactical case study**. Your execs love the data. Your analysts love the patterns. And your attackers? They hate that you **can now predict their next move**.

21. Scalability is never an issue. ATP adapts to environments large and small—from a few dozen endpoints to multinational, distributed data centers. It doesn't choke under sample loads or stall during peak hours. It was designed to grow with your network, not act like a clunky appliance stuck in 2012. Cloud-native in spirit and optimized for high throughput, ATP's ninja stars are **as endless as your expansion plans**.

22. ATP doesn't replace your firewall—it empowers it. Suddenly, your SRX isn't just enforcing policy—it's doing threat reconnaissance, behavioral analysis, and dynamic adaptation. It becomes a sentinel that can observe, react, and counter with surgical precision. Instead of reacting after the breach, you're now **counterpunching before it lands**. With ATP, the firewall evolves from static guard to **strategic weapon**.

23. If your SOC is the brain of your security operations, ATP is its third eye—**scanning beyond what's visible, predicting what's probable, and responding before it's painful**. It reduces alert fatigue by filtering noise. It automates remediation by trusting behavior. And it enhances decision-making with context only an AI-assisted threat engine could deliver. That's not just a win. That's **enlightened defense**.

24. What separates ATP from traditional sandboxes or scanning services is its **relentless adaptability**. The more you feed it, the sharper it gets. The more attacks it sees, the more likely it is to block novel ones. It's the firewall feature that thinks, learns, and protects like a battle-hardened warrior. The longer it stays in your stack, the more invincible you become. That's **legacy-grade protection wrapped in a next-gen cloak**.

25. So when your boss asks how your network is defending against the unknown, don't talk about ports or patch cycles. Talk about **Advanced Threat Protection — Juniper's ninja stars**. Talk about behavioral learning, real-time blocking, sandbox mastery, and self-updating threat IQ. Let them know the next attack won't just be stopped — it'll be studied, taught, and used as training fuel. And then point at your SRX and say, "It's not a firewall anymore. It's **a dojo with claws**."

Chapter 21: Sky ATP – Cloud-Level Shuriken Tossing

1. If Advanced Threat Protection is the ninja toolkit, then **Sky ATP** is the **cloud dojo in the sky**, where malware gets roundhouse kicked out of your network by digital senseis. It's not just a backend service — it's the **cloud brain of Juniper's defense matrix**, constantly scanning, learning, and launching security shuriken at threats as they cross your digital threshold. Think of it as the eye in the sky that watches over your SRX firewalls, vSRXs, and cSRXs like a wise old master. But make no mistake — Sky ATP isn't just observing. It's actively **profiling, detonating, correlating, and avenging your packets**. And just like any skilled ninja, it never sleeps. It just studies malware like it's prepping for a sparring match.

2. Sky ATP was built for scale. It analyzes billions of files, URLs, and connections from networks all over the world. When your SRX encounters something suspicious — a file download, a strange IP, a sketchy domain — it doesn't panic. It politely hands that payload to Sky ATP, which then **unleashes a battery of analysis engines, sandbox tools, and threat detectors** on it. If the file misbehaves in its digital dojo, it gets flagged, logged, and banned. If it's clean, it's returned with a thumbs-up. Verdicts are fast, accurate, and piped right back into your firewall **like cybernetic muscle memory**.

3. The magic of Sky ATP lies in its **multi-stage detection engine**. First, static analysis checks hashes and known signatures at lightspeed. Then, metadata is scanned to look for suspicious patterns. If that doesn't settle the score, the file is **detonated in a sandbox**, where Sky ATP watches it like a hawk in a kendo match. It logs every call, every memory write, every connection attempt. It doesn't care what the malware *says* it's doing. It cares what it **actually tries to do**. And once that intel is gathered, Sky ATP updates its cloud knowledgebase — and your firewall's IQ — with real-time results.

4. What sets Sky ATP apart is its **use of behavior-based learning and machine learning models**, trained on real-world malware patterns. It's not just about looking for known indicators. It's about watching how things behave when no one's looking. Wanna-be ransomware that copies itself to temp directories, makes DNS calls to weird domains, and starts scanning for network shares? Sky ATP sees it coming. Malicious PDFs that execute PowerShell in the background? Toast. Malware pretending to be clean? **Caught mid-lie by a well-timed sandbox sweep**.

5. Sky ATP doesn't work in isolation—it's the **neural network that empowers your entire Juniper stack**. SRX devices send samples and get verdicts. Security Director Cloud visualizes those verdicts and lets you build dynamic policies. And your SecIntel feeds get populated with the freshest, most furious threat intelligence from Sky ATP's constant cloud warfare. Your entire network becomes part of a bigger cyber-ninja clan, trained and ready for war. You're not alone. You're part of a **cloud-scale defense league with instant intel and automatic reflexes**.

6. Verdicts from Sky ATP aren't vague. They're laser-focused: malicious, suspicious, benign. And each one comes with logs, behavior traces, risk scores, and action recommendations. It's like getting a scroll with the enemy's name, weapons, tactics, and favorite hiding spots. Your firewall can act instantly—blocking traffic, dropping connections, alerting admins, or sharing intel with your SIEM. This isn't just policy—it's **precision-guided counteroffensive**.

7. Sky ATP also shines at **file reputation management**. Common files are recognized and cleared instantly—no delay, no sandbox. New or rare files get full-spectrum analysis. You can whitelist known-good files, blacklist repeat offenders, and feed this intel into broader security systems. Whether it's a sketchy executable or a seemingly innocent Excel macro, Sky ATP handles it with **the suspicion of a jaded ninja who's seen it all**.

8. URLs and DNS requests aren't exempt. Sky ATP scans them too, matching against malicious site databases, command-and-control indicators, and domain behavior profiles. If a user clicks a phishing link, Sky ATP can detect, dissect, and disable that threat before it lands. Cloud services don't get a free pass either. SharePoint downloads, Dropbox links, SaaS attachments—**all under surveillance**. Because your data may be floating in the sky, but **your protection stays grounded and focused**.

9. Sky ATP integrates beautifully with **SSL inspection workflows**, ensuring that encrypted threats don't get a free ride. Files inside HTTPS sessions are decrypted, analyzed, and sanitized mid-flight. The user doesn't notice, but the firewall does. And Sky ATP watches from above, confirming payloads with real-time detonation. You're not breaking trust—you're **rebuilding it with layered inspection and cloud insight**.

10. The platform is also deeply **API-driven**, allowing integration with SOAR platforms, SIEMs, EDR tools, and custom dashboards. You can query for verdicts, pull IOC feeds, retrieve sandbox videos, or automate incident responses—all through secure, well-documented endpoints. It turns threat intelligence into **programmable defense**, available to every app in your ecosystem. The cloud isn't a mystery anymore—it's your ally.

11. Sky ATP also respects **regional data handling laws**, with options for EU data residency and compliance controls. You don't have to sacrifice legal clarity for cloud-scale performance. Files are analyzed with strict metadata boundaries and audit trails. You'll know who submitted what, where it was inspected, and how it was judged. Even your legal team will breathe a little easier, knowing your **ninja squad fights clean**.

12. Visualization is where Sky ATP gets stylish. Dashboards in Security Director Cloud show threat heatmaps, sandbox verdicts, kill chains, file origins, and time-based analytics. Want to track a malware campaign over time? Easy. Need to see which users downloaded suspicious files? Two clicks. Sky ATP gives you **x-ray goggles for your firewall's threat history**, so you don't just react—you **understand your battlefield**.

13. If you're into threat hunting, Sky ATP is your scouting tool. Search for samples, IPs, URLs, domains, or behavioral patterns. See what matched, when it hit, and how it was stopped. Then use that info to harden your policies or preemptively block entire categories of risk. Sky ATP doesn't just fight the last war—it **prevents the next one**. And when you're ready, it shows you how to turn offense into layered defense.

14. For DevOps and SecOps alike, Sky ATP is **zero-maintenance magic**. There's no box to patch. No OS to reboot. Just seamless cloud updates, always-on learning, and threat intel that never ages. You focus on defending your apps. It focuses on **detecting what you haven't seen yet**. The result? Time saved, breaches prevented, and **threats sliced midair**.

15. So here's to Sky ATP: the cloud ninja master that never misses a throw. It watches your traffic from above, studies your threats with ancient wisdom, and responds with new-world reflex. You don't install it—you **summon it**. And when it appears, malware doesn't stand a chance. Just a whisper, a verdict, and a vanished payload. That's **shuriken-grade security, delivered from the sky**.

17. Sky ATP's reach goes beyond your own borders—it participates in a **global threat collective**, learning from organizations across industries and continents. When a new threat appears in one country, Sky ATP can intercept it elsewhere **in milliseconds**. It's like a planetary early warning system, quietly distributing digital shurikens across firewalls around the world. You don't need to be the first to spot a threat to be the first to block it. Sky ATP makes your network smarter by learning from **everyone else's near-misses**. It's the strength of many, unified in one platform. And that's some serious network ninjutsu.

18. For managed service providers and large enterprises, Sky ATP offers **multi-tenant visibility**, letting each tenant view their own threats while administrators oversee the entire fleet. It's scalable, compartmentalized security intelligence, with granular role-based access and clean reporting lines. Each team gets exactly what they need—**no more, no less**. And the centralized dashboards ensure no tenant becomes a blind spot. Whether you're defending twenty users or twenty thousand, Sky ATP scales its insight like a grandmaster scaling a mountain—**with steady, silent force**.

19. Let's not forget the **sandbox videos**, one of the most underrated features of Sky ATP. Want to see malware behavior in real time? You can watch it—literally—doing its dirty work in a virtual machine: clicking through fake screens, dropping files, and calling home to sketchy servers. It's one thing to read a verdict. It's another thing to **watch the enemy in action**, like reviewing sparring tape before a tournament. No assumptions, no ambiguity—just visual proof that your firewall made the right call.

20. Sky ATP can also **accelerate investigations and incident response**. With powerful query tools, analysts can trace malware back to source, identify impacted users, and deploy countermeasures—all from a single portal. What used to take hours of log correlation and alert triage now takes minutes. And while your security team does their part, Sky ATP continues to scout ahead—**a forward sentinel for your digital castle**.

21. With every upload, Sky ATP refines its intelligence engine. It doesn't just memorize patterns —it **synthesizes attack methods**, learns from failed attempts, and adjusts detection logic on the fly. It's like a sensei who never stops training, always refining the next kata. Attackers evolve? So does your defense. There's no manual update to wait for. Just continuous protection that **evolves while you sleep**.

22. For compliance teams, Sky ATP logs everything with meticulous clarity. Every scan, verdict, timestamp, file origin, sandbox session—it's all recorded, searchable, exportable. Whether you need a monthly audit report or a line-by-line forensic breakdown, the data is **at your fingertips**. And the peace of mind that brings to a compliance review? Priceless. You don't just meet regulations—you leap over them in a spinning backflip.

23. Admins also gain **policy-building agility** with the intel Sky ATP provides. Once you know which threats are trending, which files are misbehaving, and which users are unlucky clickers, you can tweak security postures proactively. Build custom rules, shift enforcement zones, or drop blocklists like a ninja setting traps in the bamboo. Your network doesn't just get safer—it gets **smarter by design**.

24. When combined with Juniper's broader ecosystem—SecIntel, Security Director Cloud, and unified policies—Sky ATP becomes more than detection. It becomes **predictive force**, threading together awareness, action, and assurance across your infrastructure. Suddenly your SRXs don't just inspect. They **preempt**. Your logs aren't just records. They're **threat blueprints**. And Sky ATP is the architect behind it all.

25. So next time someone asks what makes Juniper different in the cloud-security world, you just smile, point skyward, and say, "**We throw shurikens from orbit.**" Because that's what Sky ATP is—a silent guardian, a cloud-forged hunter, and the ninja you never see… until it's already neutralized the threat.

Chapter 22: SecIntel – Knowledge Is Ninja Power

1. In the ninja arts, knowledge is power—but in Juniper's security world, **SecIntel is the power behind the punch**. It's not a flashy tool. It doesn't throw shurikens. It doesn't run sandbox detonations. What it does is **feed your network's defenses with the freshest, deadliest threat intelligence**—silently, consistently, and scalably. It's the scroll of secret knowledge your firewall reads before striking. Whether it's a list of known bad IPs, malicious domains, or hash signatures of shady files, SecIntel ensures your defenses act **before the attack even lands**. It's like knowing the enemy's move before they throw the first punch.

2. At its core, SecIntel is Juniper's **curated threat feed delivery engine**, integrating seamlessly with SRX firewalls and Security Director. It provides pre-vetted, constantly updated lists of malicious indicators, including C2 servers, known malware hosts, botnet IPs, and more. You don't need to pull threat intel manually or rely on outdated spreadsheets. Your devices get the freshest intel **automagically**—like a ninja receiving coded messages in the night. With SecIntel enabled, your firewall isn't just enforcing policy—it's making **informed, real-time kill decisions** based on global threat awareness.

3. SecIntel works by integrating threat feeds directly into **JunOS policies,** allowing for lightning-fast lookups at packet processing time. These feeds are processed in hardware, using custom ASICs and flow engines, so you can block thousands of IPs or domains without a performance hit. It's like having a hit list etched into your firewall's muscle memory. Each packet is scanned against the intel. If there's a match, the response is instant—drop, deny, alert, or quarantine. No hesitation. No need for deep analysis. Just **clean cuts, ninja-style**.

4. These feeds aren't just generic—they're **curated, categorized, and context-rich**. You can pick and choose the intel you want to use: ransomware sources, phishing domains, crypto-jacking IPs, or nation-state threat actors. Want to block only high-confidence indicators? Done. Need to allow some categories while alerting on others? Easy. SecIntel is **customizable without being complicated**, giving you precise control over how your firewall uses its knowledge.

5. One of the coolest features of SecIntel is its **custom feed support**. You can ingest your own threat intelligence—whether it comes from honeypots, internal forensics, commercial feeds, or a really angry intern who's been watching Wireshark for eight hours. Convert that data into Juniper-compatible format, and your firewall starts blocking based on **your intel, your rules, your terms**. It's like giving your ninja firewall its own sixth sense—tailored, honed, and loyal only to you.

6. The updates are **cloud-delivered and continuous**, ensuring that your policies evolve in real time. You don't need to push firmware updates or reboot your network. SecIntel trickles knowledge in like a whisper on the wind—always learning, always improving, and never sleeping. The moment something dangerous is seen on another network in the Juniper ecosystem, your devices learn about it too. Your defense becomes **globalized without being exposed**.

7. With SecIntel, you can **write smarter policies**. Instead of crafting complex chains of source/destination rules, you can create simple, powerful statements like "block all C2 IPs from the ransomware feed" or "alert on phishing URLs seen in the last 24 hours." That's security policy as storytelling—with SecIntel as your narrator, whispering tales of cyber enemies defeated before dawn. Less code. More meaning. **Maximum damage to the adversary.**

8. When used with **Sky ATP**, SecIntel gets even sharper. Sky ATP discovers the threats. SecIntel delivers the blocklists. Together, they form a loop of detection and prevention that grows smarter with every scan. It's the network equivalent of a dojo that trains itself based on every fight it wins. You're not just stopping today's threats—you're **arming yourself against tomorrow's ambushes**.

9. The integration with **Security Director Cloud** means SecIntel's reach extends into dashboards, visualizations, and policy builders. You can see which threats were blocked by feed, what IPs tried to slip through, and which users are clicking things they really shouldn't. Then you can take action—tighten policy, expand feeds, or write a gentle reminder that ".exe attachments from unknown senders are not your friend." It's visibility with a side of vengeance.

10. Even in environments that demand **low latency and high throughput**, SecIntel thrives. Juniper's architecture ensures these checks don't slow down traffic. Your packets glide through the firewall like a blade through silk—fast, clean, precise. And if one matches a feed? It's gone before the user even notices. That's **true zero-delay enforcement**, not just marketing spin.

11. For security analysts and SOC teams, SecIntel is a **source of confidence**. It reduces alert fatigue by cutting off known threats early. It gives context for blocked connections. It simplifies investigation, because "blocked by threat feed" is way easier to explain than "maybe this IP is bad, not sure, we'll check later." The logs don't lie. They **just drop packets and move on**.

12. In highly segmented environments, SecIntel also enables **differentiated security postures**. You can apply certain feeds to specific zones—maybe your finance department blocks more aggressively, while R&D just gets alerts. Each zone becomes its own dojo, with its own wisdom, its own tactics, and its own layered knowledge. And the best part? You manage it all from a single, centralized brain.

13. Some might ask—why not just use open-source feeds or free blacklists? And sure, you can. But SecIntel offers **curation, support, validation, and performance optimization**—not to mention the native Juniper integration. You're not duct-taping a ninja star to a tennis racket. You're wielding a finely balanced blade, built specifically for this kind of battle.

14. Threat intel is only valuable if it's **fast, accurate, and actionable**. That's the triad SecIntel nails. And in a world where new threats emerge hourly, having automated, pre-filtered, ready-to-enforce data is the difference between sweating in a war room and sipping matcha while your firewall **disposes of the enemy like clockwork**.

15. And when the threats change—and they always do—SecIntel doesn't break stride. Feeds update, rules adjust, and your security policies evolve with no downtime, no ticket queues, and no excuses. It's the definition of agility. The firewall doesn't panic. It just acts. And SecIntel **feeds the blade**.

16. So here's to SecIntel: the quiet, all-seeing ninja scroll that arms your infrastructure with global wisdom, local context, and lightning-fast reflexes. It doesn't need to shout. It doesn't need to explode. It just needs to be there—calm, informed, and deadly precise.

17. SecIntel's power also lies in its ability to **build institutional memory into your firewall fabric**. Every blocked connection becomes part of a long-term history that your network retains.

It learns what not to trust, even if it's dressed differently next time. That rogue IP might return under a new identity—but SecIntel remembers. It's the difference between filtering traffic and **hunting for trouble like a seasoned warrior**. Knowledge isn't static—it's weaponized memory, sharpened with every packet.

18. Your threat landscape is constantly shifting, and SecIntel ensures that your security strategy stays a few steps ahead. With predictive feeds based on emerging trends and attacker patterns, you start seeing indicators **before they become headlines**. Think of it as cyber weather forecasting. When the threat storm brews, you've already fortified the castle. Your firewall isn't just reactive—it's **preemptively dangerous**.

19. Even your incident response gets a boost from SecIntel. Instead of diving through ambiguous logs, you can search threat matches, trace flow patterns, and isolate the source—quickly. There's clarity in every drop. And that makes your security team more nimble, more confident, and frankly, a lot less cranky. When you know what hit you, you can hit back harder. And SecIntel gives you that edge with **no ambiguity, no fluff**.

20. It's also worth noting that SecIntel supports **multi-vendor interoperability**. If your environment includes firewalls, routers, proxies, and endpoints from various vendors, you can still centralize your threat intel and distribute it efficiently. Juniper plays nice in a complex dojo. And with proper formatting and APIs, you can spread SecIntel like digital pollen—**cross-pollinating protection across platforms**.

21. In highly regulated industries—finance, healthcare, government—SecIntel becomes a compliance team's secret weapon. You can prove that threat intelligence is current, applied, and enforced. You can show where blocks occurred, why they happened, and how your policy responded. There's no need for interpretive dance when auditors ask about malware. Just hand them a report. And watch them nod in **respectful astonishment**.

22. When it comes to operationalizing SecIntel, the key is **integration and iteration**. Add it to your CI/CD pipeline. Tie it to your SIEM's alert logic. Build dashboard views that overlay threat blocks with business data. The more you integrate it, the more powerful it becomes. It's not just a feed. It's the **nervous system of your firewall strategy**.

23. As threats grow in sophistication, your network's defense must grow in wisdom. SecIntel ensures you're not just fast—you're smart. You act with intent, guided by knowledge from a collective cybersecurity mind. Every packet you block is a lesson learned, a battle won. And every lesson is fed back into the system for the next fight. That's how ninjas scale.

24. The best part? It's quiet. No massive GUI. No bloated dashboards. Just silent, smart filtering. The firewall doesn't brag. It **executes**. That's the spirit of SecIntel—**power through knowledge, and mastery through silence**.

25. So the next time someone scoffs at threat feeds or doubts automated defense, let them duel your firewall. Then show them the logs. Then sip your tea and remind them: **"The sharpest blades are fed by the oldest scrolls."**

Chapter 23: Contrail Security – The Silent Partner

1. Every skilled ninja has a silent partner—the one who moves in shadows, sees everything, and rarely says a word. In Juniper's world, that partner is **Contrail Security**, the quiet force behind policy enforcement in dynamic, cloud-native networks. While firewalls block and ATP detonates, Contrail Security **coordinates, maps, and maneuvers**. It doesn't throw shurikens—it **orchestrates the entire dojo**. Whether it's Kubernetes, OpenStack, VMware, or bare metal, Contrail Security brings policy awareness to where applications actually live. And that makes it the invisible backbone of your zero-trust empire.

2. Contrail Security is built on the premise that traditional perimeters are fading. Workloads shift. Containers blink in and out of existence. VMs migrate. And trying to build static security in this reality is like chasing shadows with a katana. Contrail doesn't fight the current—it flows with it, leveraging **intent-based networking, microsegmentation, and policy automation** to turn chaos into control. It doesn't guess. It doesn't panic. It observes, adapts, and **silently enforces security everywhere**.

3. At its core, Contrail Security is a **software-defined networking (SDN) solution** with deep security muscle. It builds a virtual fabric that understands workloads, tags, roles, and traffic flows. Once integrated into your cloud platform, it **maps out communication patterns, tracks dependencies, and applies microsegmented policies** based on real behavior—not just guesses or port numbers. Every pod, every VM, every NIC becomes an actor in a grand choreography of access control. And Contrail is the choreographer with a blade.

4. Microsegmentation is where Contrail really earns its ninja stars. Instead of flat, over-trusted networks, it **builds policy per app, per service, per tenant, or per tag**. Traffic only flows where it should. East-west movement is scrutinized. And even internal app components have to justify their conversations. It's like assigning every ninja their own personalized permission scroll—and enforcing it with a snare trap.

5. One of the most elegant parts of Contrail Security is **policy abstraction**. You write security rules in terms of application intent: "Web can talk to App," "App can talk to DB." You don't care about IPs or subnets. Contrail translates your intent into real-time enforcement, even as environments shift and scale. Containers restart? No problem. Nodes get replaced? Doesn't matter. Policies follow the logic—not the infrastructure. That's **security as choreography, not chaos**.

6. Contrail Security thrives in containerized environments like Kubernetes, where it integrates natively with the control plane. Every pod gets a network policy. Every namespace becomes a security zone. And every service is monitored for deviations from expected communication paths. It's like embedding a watchful monk inside each node, meditating over every packet, and **disallowing even a whisper of rogue behavior**.

7. Visibility is built-in and beautiful. Contrail Security doesn't just enforce policy—it **shows you everything**: traffic flows, service dependencies, security violations, and application heatmaps. You can zoom from global overviews down to specific containers and see exactly who talked to what, when, and why. This is not just data—it's **awareness made visual**. The map is the territory, and you are the master.

8. Real-time telemetry powers dynamic response. If a service suddenly starts behaving suspiciously—reaching out to new domains, opening strange ports—Contrail notices. It alerts. It isolates. It can even trigger automation hooks to **quarantine, log, or notify**. All without you lifting a finger. Because true mastery is silent. And **Contrail never breaks its stance**.

9. Enforcement happens in the data plane, using virtual routing and forwarding (VRF), security groups, and policy enforcement points. This means fast decisions, localized control, and **no hairpinning through central boxes**. You get scale, speed, and consistency—even across thousands of nodes. Contrail doesn't slow your network—it **sharpens it**.

10. It's also deeply API-driven, letting DevOps teams integrate policy controls into CI/CD pipelines, Infrastructure-as-Code frameworks, and GitOps flows. You can version your security just like you version code. Policies become artifacts. Workflows become secure by design. And infrastructure becomes self-defending. That's not security-as-a-service—it's **security-as-reflex**.

11. Multi-tenancy is native to Contrail. Each tenant, app, or service group can have its own isolated policy domain, RBAC, and telemetry. This makes it ideal for service providers, large enterprises, and anyone who needs fine-grained control across shared infrastructure. Your tenants don't step on each other's toes. Your apps don't fight for visibility. And your policies remain **untangled and unshakable**.

12. For hybrid and multi-cloud environments, Contrail provides **consistent policy enforcement across platforms**. You define intent once—and enforce it anywhere: AWS, Azure, GCP, on-prem, or in between. You don't need to rewire your policy logic for each provider. Contrail sees the network through the lens of abstraction and enforces it with **digital precision**.

13. One of its hidden strengths is **east-west traffic analysis**, often overlooked in traditional perimeter-based security models. Contrail tracks internal flows with the same diligence as inbound threats. This lets you spot lateral movement, shadow IT, and privilege escalation before they explode into breaches. No blind spots. Just **constant internal surveillance, without noise**.

14. Contrail Security also integrates with third-party threat intelligence, SIEMs, and analytics engines. You can export flow logs, push alerts, and feed behavior data into broader security platforms. It's not jealous. It shares. But it always remains the source of truth. In a world of overlapping toolsets, Contrail stands quietly, steadily, as **the digital spinal cord** of your defense system.

15. And when you do need to troubleshoot? Contrail's logging, flow visualization, and audit trails are deep, structured, and human-readable. You don't need to decipher logs like ancient runes. You read. You understand. You act. Security doesn't need to be mysterious. It just needs to be **effective and elegant**.

16. So here's to Contrail Security: the silent partner in your dojo of defense. It won't shout. It won't dazzle. It'll just sit in the background—mapping flows, enforcing logic, and meditating over every policy you craft. And when the attack comes, it'll be ready. Because that's what the silent ones do best.

17. Contrail's silent mastery is amplified when it's allowed to **learn and evolve from its environment**. As patterns of normal usage emerge, it can flag anomalies that even seasoned security analysts might overlook. Over time, this behavioral baseline becomes a powerful shield against zero-day attacks and insider threats. It doesn't guess—it observes and remembers. Whether it's subtle privilege escalations or rogue API calls, Contrail identifies outliers with stoic precision. It's like having a surveillance master with photographic memory—only it doesn't sleep, doesn't blink, and never forgets. That's vigilance, woven into virtual threads.

18. Developers often fear security as a friction point—but Contrail turns it into an enabler. Through its tight integration with DevOps tooling, policy gets pushed as code, not as tickets. This means faster deployments without skipping security checkpoints. It's secure velocity, wrapped in YAML and backed by silent enforcement. Developers stay focused on features while Contrail handles the guardianship. That's harmony between builders and defenders. It's not a wall—it's a **woven shield built into the blueprint**.

19. Contrail's ability to tag and label workloads makes policy granularity an art form. You can define access not by IP or VLAN, but by role, owner, app type, or even deployment tier. "Only frontend pods labeled 'prod' can talk to payment processors" becomes an enforceable truth—not a vague wishlist. These tags follow workloads across reboots, migrations, and autoscaling. So your security intent doesn't get lost in the chaos of scale. It stays sharp. Like a blade that knows exactly who it's meant to protect—and who it's meant to stop.

20. Disaster recovery and failover scenarios are no longer the nightmare they used to be. Because policies are decoupled from infrastructure, you can spin up replicas, clone environments, or roll over to another region—and security just **comes with it**. There's no rebuilding ACLs, rewriting firewall configs, or replicating subnets by hand. Contrail abstracts complexity so your recovery plan is **as silent as it is swift**. And when things go wrong, it doesn't scream—it acts, with elegant resilience. You don't react. You recover—with grace.

21. Compliance teams also benefit from Contrail's clean audit trails and declarative policy language. Every rule is traceable. Every flow is visible. Every change is logged. Whether you're chasing PCI, HIPAA, or just trying to sleep better at night, Contrail turns audits into tea ceremonies—ritual, quiet, and handled with care. No frantic searching. Just elegant records, arranged like petals on a pond.

22. Even your zero-trust journey gets a head start. With identity-based access, behavior tracking, and policy enforcement at the workload level, Contrail becomes your **trust-but-verify engine**. Lateral movement? Shut down. Unauthorized calls? Blocked. And privileged paths? Guarded with microsegmented purpose. It's not about denying access—it's about proving who should have it, and confirming that proof with every packet. That's not just security—it's **discipline, digitized**.

23. In the end, Contrail's strength isn't just in technology—it's in its philosophy. It doesn't believe in barriers. It believes in **guidance**. It doesn't believe in noise. It believes in **clarity**. And it doesn't believe in panic. It believes in **preparedness that flows with the network's rhythm**. That's why it doesn't raise alarms. It simply prevents the need.

24. With the rest of Juniper's ecosystem—ATP, SecIntel, SRX, and Mist AI—Contrail doesn't compete. It **complements**. It fills the quiet spaces between detection and enforcement. It glues intent to implementation. And it turns complex environments into understandable, actionable architectures. Think of it not as a tool—but as the pulse beneath your security posture.

25. So the next time your network feels overwhelming, sprawling, or chaotic, breathe deep. And remember: the calm, watching presence of Contrail Security is there—mapping every node, enforcing every rule, and holding the line where others guess. It's not the loudest voice. It's the **quietest certainty**. And in the world of digital defense, that's the partner you want on your side.

Chapter 24: Mist AI & Security – Enlightened Automation

1. In the realm of network security, where chaos often reigns and dashboards overflow with blinking alerts, there rises a calm voice—**Mist AI**. It's not a firewall. It's not a feed. It's a **digital sensei** that observes your entire infrastructure, anticipates problems, and helps your systems find harmony. Mist AI doesn't command—it **guides**. It transforms automation from brute force into something that feels like intuition. In Juniper's dojo of digital defense, Mist AI brings the clarity of cloud, the wisdom of analytics, and the patience of a monk. And it does it all without raising its voice.

2. Mist AI began as a wireless marvel—optimizing access points and delivering blissful Wi-Fi—but its power grew. It saw beyond the SSID, past the switches, deep into the flow of data and into **user experience itself**. Now, with the expansion of Juniper's security stack, Mist AI applies its talents to **security policy orchestration, anomaly detection, and SLEs for the secure path**. It no longer just improves connections—it **protects them with grace**. It unites SecOps with NetOps and makes sure your users are safe, satisfied, and not secretly suffering through packet loss. It's no longer just Wi-Fi zen—it's **network enlightenment from edge to core**.

3. Where other AI tools are black boxes wrapped in buzzwords, Mist AI is delightfully transparent. It shows you what it's doing, why it's doing it, and what you can do to refine its wisdom. Its **Marvis virtual network assistant** doesn't just surface alerts—it offers **answers**, complete with historical context, recommended actions, and confidence ratings. You're not talking to a log parser—you're speaking to a digital strategist. If a user has issues connecting, Marvis knows. If a new device is behaving suspiciously, Mist AI sees it. And if your policies are starting to conflict, it tells you—in a conversational tone that feels more helpful than haughty.

4. Mist AI is deeply rooted in **data correlation**. It pulls metrics from access points, switches, firewalls, and cloud-based threat engines to form a **unified view of service quality and security posture**. Every decision it makes is grounded in real evidence—latency, DNS lookup times, authentication failures, SNR, application health, and more. It then applies machine learning models, trained on **millions of datapoints across thousands of networks**, to spot what's normal —and what isn't. This lets it surface subtle problems before humans would ever see them. And once those problems are detected, it suggests or even automates **surgical responses**, not sweeping changes. It's like having a kung-fu master for every packet.

5. The security features powered by Mist AI are not bolted-on—they're **baked into the architecture**. Juniper's SRX firewalls and EX/QFX switches send telemetry directly to Mist Cloud, where it's contextualized and interpreted for intent. Mist AI can detect when traffic deviates from policy, when unknown applications begin transmitting data, or when a new device exhibits rogue behavior. It doesn't panic—it **analyzes and adapts**. It offers security SLEs— Service Level Expectations—that track metrics like threat detection efficacy and policy compliance. Then it maps those expectations to real-world usage and shows you where policy gaps are creating vulnerability valleys. It's a blend of logic and awareness that **feels suspiciously like wisdom**.

6. When integrated with **Security Director Cloud**, Mist AI becomes the conductor of a symphony. It doesn't manage policy line by line—it **harmonizes them across your entire environment**. Think of thousands of intent-based rules, flowing between users, devices, apps, and cloud services—coordinated like a tai chi master flowing through a kata. There's no chaos— just fluid enforcement. If rules begin to conflict, Mist AI spots the inconsistency. If flows begin to suffer due to overly aggressive controls, it recommends restraint. And if you're overwhelmed, Mist AI becomes your **decision partner in silence**.

7. One of Mist AI's most beloved powers is **Self-Driving Network Automation**. When thresholds are breached, changes can be enacted automatically—without the need for frantic keyboard mashing. These automations aren't blind—they're based on confidence levels, impact analysis, and user-defined policy thresholds. This means no unexpected shutdowns, no "oops" moments, and no debugging marathons in the middle of a Sunday BBQ. You can audit every action, approve before deployment, or let Mist act freely based on profile confidence. It's not autopilot—it's **augmented intuition for the digital battlefield**. Mist AI doesn't replace you. It **removes the drudgery so you can focus on the strategy**.

8. Endpoint visibility is also a core strength. Mist AI can profile and track every connected client —IoT, BYOD, rogue, or VIP. It uses MAC addresses, DNS queries, behavioral fingerprints, and contextual metadata to **build a complete picture of device behavior over time**. If a smart thermostat starts talking to Russia, you'll know. If a rogue switch gets plugged in behind a printer, Mist AI has the receipts. And if someone brings in a "gaming rig" disguised as a work laptop, you'll see it labeled, flagged, and optionally quarantined. It's full-spectrum, end-to-end **awareness without the tedium**.

9. Troubleshooting is perhaps where Mist AI brings the most serenity. Traditional methods demand pings, traceroutes, and finger-pointing between teams. Mist AI just tells you—**"This user experienced packet loss from 2:47 to 2:51 PM due to a DHCP conflict on AP-3, now**

resolved." No guessing. No shouting. No war rooms. Just clarity. Delivered in plain language and visualized with precision.

10. But the true magic comes from how Mist AI **learns over time**. Every fix, feedback loop, and deployment helps refine its models. It becomes your institutional memory—knowing which policies succeed, which devices misbehave, and which workloads cause friction. Over time, your environment stops feeling like a patchwork and starts feeling like **a dojo**—balanced, responsive, and intentional. You don't configure anymore. You **collaborate**. And Mist AI becomes not just a tool, but a **guardian spirit**.

11. Compliance auditing is made easier by Mist AI's detailed event logging and intuitive dashboards. You don't need to scramble for packet captures or craft narratives from vague logs. Every alert, action, policy decision, and anomaly is **stored, timestamped, and categorized for easy export**. PCI-DSS, HIPAA, ISO 27001—they're all easier when you can show a dashboard that practically narrates your security tale. Mist doesn't just meet compliance. It **transforms it into a daily discipline**—without the headache.

12. With the rise of AI-based threats, Mist AI doesn't get caught off guard—it's **already on the path of evolution**. As attackers use automation and obfuscation, Mist AI learns to spot synthetic anomalies—patterns too perfect to be human. It watches for machine-speed reconnaissance, strange token usage, and fake behavioral mimicry. Where old tools might miss subtle pattern deviation, Mist AI catches it in the rhythm of the flow. It's not just reactive—it's **introspective, perceptive, and a few milliseconds ahead**. In the coming age of automated cyber warfare, Mist isn't your last line—it's your **first defender**.

13. The user experience is where Mist AI breaks from every clunky tool you've ever known. Everything lives in a single UI—polished, purposeful, and elegantly designed. You don't need 14 tabs and an Excel sheet to manage a wireless policy or trace a firewall event. Mist AI pulls it all together, displaying your entire environment as a **living, breathing security story**. From the moment a packet arrives to the instant it's blocked or passed, the context is captured and displayed in a way that even your CEO could understand. That's not dumbing it down—it's **elevating the signal and silencing the noise**.

14. Mist AI doesn't care if your infrastructure is all Juniper or a multi-vendor mashup. Through open APIs, telemetry standards, and a firm belief in **interoperability**, it fits into complex environments with ease. Whether you have Cisco switches, Palo Alto firewalls, or legacy access points, Mist AI can still ingest, interpret, and improve what's already there. It doesn't demand you throw away the old—it simply **enlightens it**. That's not replacement—that's **network nirvana through augmentation**.

15. So here's to Mist AI: the enlightened automation engine, the digital guardian monk, the sensei of self-driving network serenity. It doesn't fight fire with fire. It fights fire with **foresight, finesse, and fairness**. Your alerts don't scream anymore—they whisper guidance. Your tickets don't pile up—they dissolve into insights. And your infrastructure? It breathes. Calm. Aware. Ready.

16. Mist AI's predictive modeling doesn't stop at today's patterns — it projects future behavior. By continuously monitoring device, application, and traffic data, it forecasts where issues are likely to appear next. Think of it as cloud-born premonition backed by statistics and machine learning. This allows teams to take proactive steps, from bandwidth shifts to rule tuning, before users even notice a slowdown. It's a strategy born not from guesswork, but from **data-driven tranquility**. In this way, Mist AI isn't just managing your network — it's **teaching it to anticipate**. And the more you let it learn, the less you'll find yourself reacting in a crisis.

17. A powerful feature of Mist AI is its ability to **guide network design evolution**. It doesn't just optimize the existing layout — it helps you plan better topology based on usage, coverage, and historical flow patterns. Want to know if a particular VLAN needs splitting? Mist will tell you. Need to segment an IoT network from production? Mist already noticed the chatter. With Mist's help, your security becomes an evolving art — refined in layers and never rigid. It's security architecture through **continuous enlightenment**. And the best part? It feels less like work and more like wisdom unfolding.

18. For IT teams tired of root cause roulette, Mist AI is a blessing. Every problem, every failure, every unexpected spike becomes a lesson. Its memory is meticulous, its logic unemotional, and its conclusions surgical. You don't waste time finger-pointing — you **see the truth, then fix the truth**. Whether it's a misconfigured firewall rule or a chatty app gone rogue, Mist gently surfaces the answer. And it does so while respecting your time, your experience, and your sanity. It's not a blamer — it's **a balancer**.

19. Mist AI also helps **optimize team collaboration** across network, security, and helpdesk roles. Its dashboards serve as shared reference points — one truth, many perspectives. This avoids tribal knowledge silos and reduces friction during triage. Everyone's reading from the same map, interpreting the same flow, acting on the same root cause. The result is faster mean-time-to-resolution, less inter-department drama, and a general aura of "we've got this." That's not just automation — it's **alignment through shared visibility**. Mist doesn't just fix issues. It fixes teamwork.

20. As remote work continues to stretch enterprise perimeters, Mist AI ensures security follows **wherever the users go**. Whether it's a coffee shop Zoom call, a VPN-less SASE connection, or a full-blown branch deployment, Mist brings SLEs and security enforcement to the edge. It doesn't lose sight of users just because they changed locations. Through cloud-native architecture and persistent telemetry, it holds onto trust context wherever the endpoint roams. This means consistent policy, sustained performance, and full threat visibility — from HQ to hammock. It's not remote access. It's **serene connectivity without compromise**.

21. If you're into automation scripts, Mist offers **intelligent integrations** with APIs, webhooks, and tools like Slack, Teams, and ServiceNow. But what makes them intelligent isn't the connection — it's the context. Mist knows not just that something broke, but why, when, and whether it needs to alert a human. This keeps your humans focused on high-value decisions, not repetitive remediation. That's digital delegation done right. Mist isn't trying to replace your team — it's making sure they spend their time like ninjas, not gophers. You script the logic. Mist adds the insight.

22. Mist AI is also designed with **privacy and ethics in mind**. It anonymizes personal data, limits exposure, and supports granular role-based access to insights. In a time when AI raises big questions, Mist answers with transparency, control, and built-in compliance support. It's a guardian that knows the line between vigilant and invasive. You see what you need, when you need it—nothing more. That's the trust layer underneath the trust policy. It's not just intelligent. It's **mindful**.

23. Network security has always been a battlefield—but Mist AI turns it into a practice. Not a war room. A **training ground**. You don't harden your systems with fire—you temper them with clarity. Every incident becomes a kata. Every alert is a bell, not a bomb. And every new insight moves your team closer to mastery.

24. Mist AI isn't just about packet inspection or firewall orchestration—it's about **awareness without noise**. It gives you a high-resolution view of cause and effect without drowning in false positives. It helps you act fast when it matters, and stay quiet when it doesn't. It doesn't default to drama. It defaults to **discernment**. And in a world full of overreaction, that's not just refreshing—it's revolutionary.

25. So bow deeply to Mist AI—the sensor, the scribe, the silent strategist. In a field obsessed with flashing lights and brute force, Mist chooses elegance, intelligence, and subtlety. It's not trying to be loud. It's trying to be right. And as it guides your network to a place of awareness, balance, and protection, it leaves you not just safer—but **wiser**. That's not just automation. That's **enlightenment, encoded**.

Chapter 25: The Future of Juniper Jitsu – What's in the Scrolls Ahead?

1. Every ninja journey ends with a reflection—not just on the battles won, but on the paths yet untrodden. In the realm of Juniper Jitsu, where intrusion detection meets introspection, the scrolls don't close—they **evolve**. As networks grow smarter, more complex, and more distributed, Juniper's security vision sharpens like a katana before dawn. We've scaled hardware fortresses, danced with virtual firewalls, and invoked AI senseis. But the true mark of a digital warrior isn't mastery of the current—it's **readiness for the uncertain**. The next threat isn't a matter of "if." It's a matter of "when and how weird."

2. One clear truth echoes across the dojo: **AI and ML aren't optional—they're central**. Mist AI was just the beginning. Expect deeper integration between AI systems and policy engines, where threat detection is not just reactive, but **anticipatory**. Behavioral analytics will expand from endpoints to entire workloads, entire campuses, and even entire industries. Patterns will be learned, threats predicted, and countermeasures tailored before the first packet pings. You won't just respond faster—you'll **pre-flect**. And that's where Juniper is placing its next bets.

3. On the hardware side, Juniper's next-generation SRX devices will be sleeker, smarter, and **deeply software-defined**. Expect zero-touch provisioning, container-native firewall modules, and a tighter marriage between control and data planes. Think of it as dojo discipline baked directly into silicon. The line between physical and virtual will blur, with hybrid firewalls that adjust power and posture based on what you're protecting. In the future, your firewall might not sit in a rack—it might live in a **microservice mesh**, doing splits across clouds with style.

4. Speaking of clouds, Juniper's Security-as-a-Service offerings will continue to **unroll across the sky**. Already with Sky ATP and Security Director Cloud, the blueprint is drawn: elastic policy, elastic intelligence, **elastic serenity**. You won't deploy software—you'll summon it. From threat feeds to enforcement logic, the cloud will become not a destination, but a **ninja's utility belt**. Need DLP on a branch office? Flick. Need segmentation for 400 pods? Flick. Need insights without alerts that scream at you? Flick. The scrolls will live in the ether—and they will be **sharp**.

5. Policy management is evolving from art to science—more precisely, to **intent-driven orchestration**. Gone are the days of if-then-else logic stacked like unsteady towers. You'll declare what you want ("Protect the dev cluster from anything not tagged 'R&D'") and the system will **interpret, deploy, and enforce it across all layers**. We're entering an age where policy is less about syntax and more about **semantics**. Firewalls won't just block—they'll reason. And Juniper is building toward an era of **semantic security**, where your intent echoes through switches, routers, sensors, and yes—even through AI ears.

6. With the rise of IoT and edge devices, visibility becomes not just a perk—it's a **pillar**. Juniper Jitsu will continue sharpening its gaze across countless endpoints: drones, cameras, thermostats, vending machines, and other mischievous byte-burglars. Detection won't come from signatures but from **silhouettes of intent**—watching devices for sudden shifts, forbidden whispers, and behavior that's just *a little too curious*. Zero trust will become zero assumptions. And firewalls will not just protect the edge—they will **become it**.

7. Collaboration across ecosystems will shape the next scrolls of integration. Expect Juniper to deepen its alliances—open APIs, enriched telemetry feeds, cross-vendor orchestration, and **shared threat vocabularies**. It's not about locking you into a single box—it's about building a symphony with your existing stack. You'll see Mist AI exchange insights with third-party SIEMs. You'll see SecIntel powering adjacent security platforms. And you'll see a shift from "vendor lock-in" to **vendor kung fu**—flexible, adaptable, and always collaborative.

8. The future also demands **human-centric design**. No more arcane CLIs for every operation. Juniper Jitsu will emphasize intuitive UIs, explainable AI, and security workflows that feel like smooth sparring—not bureaucratic belt tests. Automation will be approachable. Insights will be visual. And your security dashboard won't look like a spaceship console—it'll look like **an enlightened dojo wall**, with clarity painted into every alert.

9. Training and certification will evolve too. Juniper's education platforms will focus on not just how to configure a device—but on how to **think like a ninja**. Expect modular learning, AI-powered testing, gamified simulations, and real-world threat labs. Your training won't end with a badge—it'll come with a scroll, a path, and a purpose. You won't just pass a test. You'll pass into **a new level of awareness**.

10. Perhaps most importantly, Juniper Jitsu is committed to ethical tech. As AI grows stronger, and as firewalls become self-aware (well, almost), principles of transparency, privacy, and trust must remain at the core. Juniper will continue to build tools that don't just secure networks—but protect **the humans who live within them**. The strongest defense is not domination—it's **disciplined empowerment**. And in the years to come, that may be the most powerful scroll of all.

11. So what's next for you, dear reader? Whether you're an overworked SOC analyst, a curious sysadmin, or a wide-eyed student who just discovered NAT—your journey continues. This book might end, but your dojo opens wider every time you SSH into a device, tweak a policy, or stare down a malformed packet. You are the next generation of Juniper Jitsu. And the scrolls you write will guide future ninjas. Go forth, wield your CLI wisely, and may your logs be **free of mystery**.

12. The future isn't static—it's **packet-shaped, AI-sculpted, and scroll-fed**. It hums in cloud regions. It whispers in Kubernetes clusters. It meditates inside Marvis's brain. And it waits for you—not to fear it, but to shape it. Your network is your dojo. The tools are in your hands. The scrolls ahead? Still unwritten.

13. As threat actors grow bolder and breaches become more sophisticated, your resilience will hinge on **adaptive choreography**, not brute force. Juniper's evolving toolsets will help you dance between detection, automation, remediation, and insight—gracefully, not reactively. This will mean building policies like movements in a kata: structured, purposeful, and fluid under pressure. Mist AI will choreograph detection. Contrail will pivot microsegmentation. Sky ATP will strike with precision. And you? You'll glide between it all like a digital shinobi.

14. SASE—Secure Access Service Edge—will continue to blur the lines between WAN, security, and identity. Juniper's cloud-delivered architecture will harmonize remote work, edge access, and threat prevention into a **single rhythm of control**. Mist AI will unify the experience. SRX will enforce. Security Director Cloud will orchestrate. Identity will no longer be an add-on—it will be the **keystone of your castle gates**. Users, devices, apps—all will move securely, even when no one's watching. And your perimeter will follow them like a shadow.

15. Expect more automation—but not less responsibility. Juniper Jitsu in the future isn't about replacing operators—it's about **refining them into masters**. AI will take away the noise. Humans will bring the nuance. Together, they'll fight threats with insight and execution, not exhaustion. Training will focus on logic, ethics, and visibility—not just syntax. The warrior of tomorrow won't memorize commands—they'll **compose intentions**.

16. Visualization will enter a new era, where your security data becomes **art in motion**. Interactive maps will illustrate packet flow like brushstrokes across a digital canvas. Alerts will morph into animated path analysis, drawing lines between compromise and containment. It won't just be data—it'll be a **story you can read in real-time**. And those stories will help you teach, share, and evolve faster than any manual ever could. Welcome to the age of **living documentation**. Powered by Mist. Read by ninjas.

17. Juniper's roadmap includes a **digital twin for your network**, where your entire infrastructure is simulated in the cloud for preemptive analysis and configuration testing. Think of it as sparring with yourself—without breaking a sweat or a system. Policy changes can be trialed. Threat models can be run. Risk can be assessed without the risk. That's not just proactive security. That's **security as rehearsal**.

18. Telemetry will evolve into **telepathy**—not quite mind-reading, but close. Granular, real-time feedback from every device, user, and process will be processed into intuitive summaries and projected forecasts. You won't have to hunt for insights. They'll arrive, wrapped in context, and whispering predictions about what's next. If you've ever wanted your network to feel alive, self-aware, and strangely helpful—Mist AI is the path. It's not magic. It's **machine wisdom wrapped in trust**.

19. Community and collaboration will be key pillars of Juniper Jitsu's next chapter. Expect open-source plugins, curated threat sharing, and dojo-style mentorship circles across the globe. Juniper won't just offer gear—it will host conversations, challenges, and codeathons. The next big threat won't be stopped by one ninja—it will take a **clan**. And together, you'll codify your scrolls as culture, not just config. What used to be silos will become **training halls of shared purpose**.

20. Sustainability will step forward too. Expect Juniper to lead with **green firewalls**, eco-conscious cloud practices, and lifecycle transparency that makes every watt count. Efficiency will no longer be a hidden bonus—it'll be part of the mission. Cooling, scaling, and component reuse will be built into the product vision, not duct-taped on afterward. Even your audit reports will glow with less carbon shame. Because saving the world should mean securing it **and not overheating it**.

21. The hybrid future will merge identity, intent, and infrastructure into one living mesh. Firewalls won't just enforce—they'll empathize. Policies will feel less like walls and more like **conductors of safe flow**. Whether you're securing a VR surgery suite or a smart farm of tractors, Juniper Jitsu will evolve to read context and apply **proportionate response**. Threats will be subtle, responses will be smoother. And the network will become something closer to intuition—built on trust, not just tickets.

22. Your CLI skills will still matter—but they'll live alongside AI whispering best practices, policy spellcheckers, and SASE graph visualizers. You'll be as likely to say "show me a packet's journey" as "show interfaces terse." And both will work. Whether you want tabs or terminal, you'll find the same strength underneath. The tools will change. The thinking will deepen. And your **ninjutsu will only sharpen**.

23. As security threats become social, political, and environmental in impact, your role will stretch. You won't just guard servers—you'll **protect institutions**. Hospitals. Schools. Newsrooms. Entire regions. Juniper Jitsu won't just be about availability—it will be about **integrity and impact**. And when history writes its next scroll, may it record: the network was strong. The guardians were wiser.

24. In the end, Juniper Jitsu isn't about the hardware, the cloud, or even the AI. It's about you—your judgment, your discipline, your willingness to learn. The tools are scrolls. The training is ongoing. The philosophy is **layered defense, delivered with clarity and calm**. And the mission? Always the same: to protect what matters, without losing your way in the noise. Let your path be silent, but strong.

25. So tie your belt, check your logs, and step lightly into the next chapter. The dojo never really closes—it simply waits for your return. With every policy you write, every alert you decode, every threat you neutralize, you write another verse in the story of **Juniper Jitsu**. From nincompoop to ninja, your journey was just the beginning. May your sessions never timeout. May your scrolls stay ever up to date. And may your enemies always wonder: **who trained you?**